Planning Horizons, Calendars and Timings in SAP APO

Shaun Snapp

Planning Horizons, Calendars and Timings in SAP APO

For information about this title or to order other books and/or electronic media, contact the publisher:
SCM Focus Press
PO Box 29502 #9059
Las Vegas, NV 89126-9502
http://www.scmfocus.com/scmfocuspress
(408) 657-0249

ISBN: 978-1-939731-00-5

Printed in the United States of America

Cover and Interior design by: 1106 Design

Contents

Contents

CHAPTER 1

Introduction

I based this book on what struck me as an interesting premise: Take four of the most commonly implemented APO applications (DP, SNP, PP/DS and GATP) and describe each of them in terms of their planning horizons and time settings, and explain the time settings of each application in relation to one another in addition to how they connect with SAP ERP.

Planning systems are filled with planning horizons, calendars and timing settings. They are all critical in controlling the behavior of these systems. I have been dealing with timing issues of this nature since I began working in advanced planning back in 1998 (first in i2 Technologies and then in APO as well as other best of breed applications such as MCA Solutions). As I look back on the many hours spent researching this topic, I can say I have never been satisfied with the documentation that has been available to me. I have gradually come to the realization that timing settings in planning systems are a topic worthy of much more emphasis both in terms of documentation as well as time spent on projects than they typically receive.

Simply describing and explaining all the system timings in one place (that is one book) would have been beneficial and an improvement over what is available on the topic. But a combined analysis of timing across the modules was a great opportunity, because I have never seen it done. System timings tend to be discussed in isolation from one another; but eventually it is necessary to move toward an integrated view of all system timings. Several chapters in this book are dedicated to cross module timings.

Why this topic?
Well, I am continually asked questions about timings within each APO module. I am also asked the more complicated question of how timing settings within each module interact with and impact upon timing settings in other modules. Clients of the large consulting companies and of SAP often complain that the consultants that work for them in each module simply go off "and do their own thing," leaving no one to answer these questions and explain the "end-to-end" process to the

client. There are several steps to defining an end-to-end process, and sometimes the expectation can be unrealistic, depending upon the stage of the project, as the end-to-end process does not simply reveal itself immediately. The first step is to define all of the functionality that will be used in an implementation. Another step is to define how users will interact with the various screens and processes in the applications. Of course, a big part of defining any end-to-end process is the planning horizons, calendars and timings that are in all of the applications.

The Detailed Nature of This Book

Of all the books I have written, this book is the most detailed, mainly due to the many time settings that exist in APO and how specific each timing setting must be defined. I found that the more I investigated timing settings, the more implications I uncovered for how they control system output. The various planning horizons in APO are probably the most obvious in this regard, but all of the timings are powerful and invariably lead to many questions during projects. I happen to know that any limitation of consulting teams to provide definitive answers on the interaction of system timings is a source of frustration for clients. As this book goes to press, this is the only published document to provide a comprehensive overview of the timings in APO.

Why a Comprehensive Timing Book is So Important for SAP APO

The need for this type of emphasis and improved documentation is particularly pressing with respect to APO. This is due to the fact that APO is the most fully featured and complicated supply chain planning suite on the market. The ways in which APO can be configured are unending, and with each new release the suite becomes even more complicated. This complexity generalizes to the timing settings, of which APO has an enormous number. No other group of applications in supply chain planning has so many fields and so many ways of being configured. This is positive in one aspect in that APO can meet the broadest number of requirements.[1] However, APO is more complex to implement than any other planning application. Due to its vast number of settings, APO has the largest potential for configuration errors and mismatches in configuration between the applications, keeping all of the timings straight, and associating the timings across the modules—as well as coordinating the timings with the connected systems—is a challenge.

Who is This Book For?

This book is for anyone who wants a better understanding of time settings in APO and other advanced planning systems, including solution architects, implementation resources, individuals that work in maintenance of APO solutions or anyone working at a company that is or plans to implement or even work with APO. Timing is such an important aspect of planning systems that the group of people who would benefit from this book is actually quite broad. However, some people may not want to make the investment to read the entire book or entire chapters, but instead use the book as a reference to be used when they have a

---

[1] Let's quickly dispense with the myth that APO (or any SAP application) can meet all customer requirements or the requirement is simply not a "best practice." This exact concept is proposed by SAP salesmen and "account managers." SAP consultants dislike this "best practices" construct as they are left with "holding the bag" on enormous best practice promises by SAP sales and account management. Just as believing in the tooth fairy past the age of ten, nothing good comes from believing in this evidence-less claim. The truth is that many practices within SAP generally (and APO specifically) are not even good practices. Secondly, many companies have custom solutions that are designed around very legitimate requirements that do not reflect how SAP happens to work. At one client, SAP told them that SNP could not meet their requirement because the way they performed deployment was not a best practice and they should change their process. Interestingly, several months later while reviewing an SAP presentation I came to find that SAP SPP was designed to meet these requirements. So which is the best practice, the deployment functionality available in SNP or the quite opposite deployment functionality available in SAP SPP? This is covered in the following article:

http://www.scmfocus.com/sapplanning/2013/01/17/saps-inconsistent-position-on-deployment/
Just because SAP does not work a particular way does not make SAP's way a best practice. At the end of the day, SAP is just another, if quite successful, software vendor. Any software vendor would like to have its customers accept the concept that they have chosen the "one best way" to do something. But there is no reason to believe them unless they bring heavy evidence and SAP doesn't. And saying "best practice" over and over again is not evidence of anything—it's merely a mantra. More on this topic can be read in the following articles:

http://www.scmfocus.com/sapprojectmanagement/2010/07/how-valid-are-saps-best-practice-claims/
http://www.scmfocus.com/sapprojectmanagement/2012/06/how-best-practices-expectations-causes-problems-on-sap-projects/

specific timing question. If you have any questions or comments on the book, email me at shaunsnapp@scmfocus.com.

Using This Book to Get a Leg Up on Timing Discussions on Projects

Because planning horizons, calendars and time settings are difficult to conceptualize until one actually sees a system where the timings have been entered, experienced consultants most often push the timing related discussions until the demo or proof of concept stage of the project, allowing the client to see how these factors influence the planning output and to make their changes after this process.

While I am in favor of placing different timings in systems and providing demonstrations of applications to clients, this method of making a decision on time settings is time consuming and relatively expensive. I am no stranger to going into unit testing with a variety of options that must be tested; however, the more that can be explained and defined prior to unit testing and integrated testing, the faster the process can be accomplished and the better its final quality. However, a significant amount of time will have passed by the time this happens. Much more can be done to make the timing issues apparent to companies before creating a demo, and I show several time-related templates in this book that provide some clarity and even a bit of consensus as to system timings.

Disclaimer About the Timing Field Definitions

This book contains many field definitions, as it covers the four modules in APO along with the considerable number of fields related to these modules. When it came to field definitions, I had to make a decision. While I needed some portions of the SAP Help definitions, I did not want to use SAP's definitions exclusively. I wanted to weave in my take on the definitions but without making the reader continually stop and start (between SAP's definition, and my definition). Therefore, I settled on using portions of the field definitions from SAP in combination with my shorthand. Some of the definitions are quite lengthy, so I have tried to provide a synopsis of them and add some translation where necessary. Because I did not want to be concerned with separating out the exact SAP quotations from my text, I am putting this disclaimer at the beginning of this book. *I am not trying to take credit for SAP's definitions, or say that any of the field definitions in this book are original*. I could have included the full definition of each field in this book, but instead opted for a synopsis as the full definition would have made the book quite tedious. The definitions are the starting point; I have included a layer of analysis and learning aids such as graphics to help clarify many of the time settings. Finally, I have not included absolutely every timing field in every category. I have covered the vast majority of them, but some are used so infrequently that I decided to leave them out of the book.

Timing Field Definitions Identification

This book is filled with lists. Some of these lists are field definitions. To help you quickly identify field definitions, all text in the field definition lists is *italicized*. In lists that are not field definitions, only the term defined is *italicized,* while the definition that follows is not italicized. Italics is really used in three places in this book:

1. Underneath screen shots

2. For field definitions

3. As further explanation which is related to field definitions.

Choosing the APO Modules for the Book

As I stated, this book only covers DP, SNP, GATP and PP/DS. If you bought this book hoping to have coverage of SPP or EWM, you will be disappointed. While the title is *Planning Horizons, Calendars and Timings in APO,* I was explicit in the description that this book included only the four modules listed, and have itemized the four modules on the cover of the book.

The reason for restricting the book to DP, SNP, GATP and PP/DS is because these are the modules most commonly implemented, and I have the most experience working with these modules. Would another book that covered all the timings in the other APO modules be helpful? Undoubtedly, but I only have so much bandwidth, so I decided to limit the scope to these four APO modules that have received the broadest implementation.

The Book Roadmap

This book can be logically divided into three sections. The first section is the individual resource timings. The second is general timing topics, which are often a source of confusion on projects. Finally, two of the last chapters fall into the integrated category, which is where the timing relationships between the APO modules, and between APO and SAP ERP are examined. This is shown in the graphic below:

Book Roadmap

Chapter Category	Module Chapters	Specialty Chapters	Integrated Chapters
Purpose	*APO Module and Resource Timings*	*Common Timing Areas Which Require Explanation*	*How The Timings Are Connected*
Chapters/Topics	CH 2. DP Planning Horizons, Calendars and Timings	CH 8. Critical Timing Topics	CH 7. Transfer Timings Between SAP APO and SAP ERP
	CH 3. SNP Planning Horizons, Calendars and Timings	CH 10. Forecast Consumption, Allocation Consumption, Scheduling Direction and Timings	CH 9. Timing Integration Between DP, SNP, PP/DS and GATP
	CH 4. PP/DS Planning Horizons, Calendars and Timings		
	CH 5. Resource Calendars and Timings		
	CH 6. GATP Planning Horizons, Calendars and Timings		

Timings Not Covered in This Book

All of the timings in this book are "within" the APO applications. However, when and how the various planning processes are triggered is another group of time-related settings. I did not cover these settings as I cover them in the book *Global Planning with SAP APO*. Beyond a single region implementation, this book tackles the complex topic of how to support a global business with a single APO application.

How Writing Bias Is Controlled at SCM Focus and SCM Focus Press

Bias is a serious problem in the enterprise software field. Large vendors receive uncritical coverage of their products, and large consulting companies recommend the large vendors with the resources to hire and pay consultants rather than the vendors with the best software for the client's needs.

Just as in my consulting practice, I do not financially benefit from a company's decision to buy an application that I showcase. SCM Focus has the most stringent rules related to controlling bias and restricting commercial influence of any information provider in the space. These "writing rules" are expressed in the link below:

  http://www.scmfocus.com/writing-rules/

If other information providers in this space followed these rules, I would be able to learn about software without being required to perform my own research and testing on every topic.

Information about enterprise supply chain planning software can be found on the Internet, but it is primarily promotional or written at such a high level that none of the important details or limitations of the application are exposed; this is true of books as well. When only one enterprise software application is covered in a book, the application works perfectly; the application operates as expected, and there are no problems during the implementation to bring the application live. This is all quite amazing and quite different from my experience of implementing enterprise software. However, it is very difficult to make a living by providing objective information about enterprise supply chain software, especially as it means being critical at some times. I once remarked to a friend that SCM Focus had very little competition in providing unvarnished information on this software category, and he said, "Of course. There is no money in it."

Making the Perfect Book for Those Hungry for Precise Information on Supply Planning Software

By writing this book, I wanted to help people get exactly the information they need without having to read a lengthy volume. The approach to the book is essentially the same as to my previous books. With that in mind, here are some of the principles I knew this book needed to follow:

1. **Be direct and concise.** There is very little theory in this book and I do not spend any time covering much more than simple math.

2. **Based on project experience.** Nothing in the book is hypothetical in that I have worked with it or tested it on an actual project. My project experience has led to understanding a number of things that are not covered in supply planning books.

3. **Saturate the book with graphics.** Roughly two-thirds of a human's sensory input is visual, and books that do not use graphics—especially educational and training books such as this one—can fall short of their purpose. Graphics have also been used consistently and extensively on the SCM Focus website.

The SCM Focus Site

I am also the author of the SCM Focus site, http://www.scmfocus.com, and therefore the site and book share a number of concepts and graphics. Furthermore, the book contains many links to articles on the site, which provide more detail on specific subjects. This book provides an explanation of how supply chain timing software works and aims to continue to be a reference after its initial reading. However, if your interest in SAP planning software continues to grow, the SCM Focus site is a good resource to which articles are continually added. The SCM site dedicated specifically to SAP planning is http://www.scmfocus.com/sapplanning.

Abbreviations

At the end of the book, there is a listing of all abbreviations used throughout the book.

CHAPTER 2

DP Planning Horizons, Calendars and Timings

Storage Buckets and Planning Buckets

DP and SNP both use the planning book, and for both a Planning Bucket Profile and Storage Bucket Profile must be set up. As the topic of the next chapter is SNP, I will discuss these profiles in detail in this chapter and only allude to them in Chapter 3: "SNP Horizons, Calendars and Timings."

As the names imply, the Planning Bucket Profile controls how the application displays the data in the planning book, and the Storage Bucket Profile controls how the application stores the planning data.

The Storage Bucket Profile, which is shared between DP and SNP, defines how often you want the data to be saved. This is the lowest level that the data will be divided into intervals in the system.

SAP has the following to say about the Storage Bucket Profile. I have placed an asterisk in front of the two most important parts of the Storage Bucket Profile:

- *One or more recurring intervals in which you wish the data to be saved.

- *The horizon during which the profile is valid.

- A time stream ID, if you wish to save the data in smaller buckets than days (this entry is optional). The time stream must be as long as or longer than the horizon. It must not be shorter than the horizon.

- The number of days, if you always want to save the data in a fixed number of rolling days at the beginning of the planning horizon, and after that in a larger bucket (this entry is optional).

Example: You select the month and week of the time periods in the Storage Buckets Profile. You do not enter a time stream. Data for the months of June and July 2000 is stored in the following buckets:

- Thursday through Sunday June 1–4 4 Days

- Monday through Sunday June 5–11 7 Days

- Monday through Sunday June 12–18 7 Days

- Monday through Sunday June 19–25 7 days

Storage Bucket Profile in the System

The Storage Bucket Profile is assigned to the planning area. The planning area is where the key figures and the key figure aggregations are set. These are the rows that eventually show in the planning book. The basic construct of the spreadsheet area of the planning book is key figures as rows (what is being reported on such as stock, forecast, etc.) and planning buckets along the top. I have included a mockup of the planning book's spreadsheet area on the following page so it's easy to follow the connection to the actual usage of key figures in APO.

Planning Book Mockup

	Key Figure Name	Common Order Categories	10/5/12	10/12/12	10/19/12
Demand	Forecast		5,000	1,000	300
	Sales Order		5,500	-	-
	Distribution Demand	Unconfirmed Purchase Requisition (either internal or external source of supply)			1,200
	Distribution Demand Confirmed	Confirmed Purchase Requisitions or Purchase Orders			
	Dependent Demand				
	Total Demand		**5,500**	**1,000**	**1,500**
Supply	Distribution Receipt	Stock Transport or Purchase Requisition			200
	Distribution Receipt Confirmed	Stock Transport Orders and Purchase Orders			
	In Transit		500		
	Production Planned		2,800	600	1,300
	Production Confirmed				
	Total Receipts		**3,300**	**600**	**1,500**
Stock	Stock on Hand		1,000	600	600
	Max Stock Level		600	600	600
	Reorder Point		500	500	500
	Safety Stock		500	300	300

This is where the Storage Bucket Profile is set up under basic settings:

Maintain Periodicity

Periodicity

Stor.Buck.Prof.   SCM Focus Storage Buck

- ☑ Day
- ☑ Week
- ☐ Month
- ☐ Quarter
- ☐ Year
- ☐ PostPeriod   Fi.Year Variant

Horizon

| Start date | 27.08.2012 |
| End Date | 12.08.2018 |

Additional Details

Time Stream ID

Time stream: External ID (1)

Restrictions

Time stream ID	
Without Gaps	
CTM Time Stream	
Long text	
Language Key	EN
Maximum No. of Hits	500

Selecting the Storage Buckets Profile brings up the screen on the following page, which allows the data to be saved in a fixed number of days at the beginning of the planning horizon and after that in a larger bucket.

Maintain Time Buckets Profile DP/SNP

[Period list] ⊚ 🗑

| Time buckets prfl ID | SCM FOCUS DAILY CTM |
| Short text | Daily CTM Run |

Time Buckets Prof. Details

Number	Basic periodicity	FYV 2	Display periodicity	FYV 1	
12			M		
6	M		W		
2	W		T		

The Planning Bucket Profile defines how the data is planned and displayed in the planning books.

The Planning Bucket Profile

After the Storage Bucket Profile has been determined, the next logical step is to configure the Planning Bucket Profile, the purpose being to define the different sections of the horizon by making entries in the columns and the display periods. The Planning Bucket Profile contains the periods or a subset of the periods that you defined in the Storage Bucket Profile. Do not include a period in the Planning Bucket Profile that is not in the Storage Bucket Profile.

These configuration steps define the future planning horizon and past horizon by entering them in a planning book—that is, duration for the future planning horizon and one for the past horizon. The future horizon starts with the smallest time bucket. The planning book must know how far in the past and how far into the future to look and to process information.

Before we adjust the planning horizons, it is a good idea to document the settings externally in a spreadsheet. By doing so, I can copy over spreadsheets from previous clients and compare and contrast different configuration and timing settings. So if we begin at the basics (i.e., what we want the Planning Bucket Profile to be), we can migrate this to SAP's information input requirements.

At the top of the next screen shot, I have placed what the Planning Bucket Profile should be in what could be called "plain English."

Planning Bucket Profile

Period	Daily Run	Weekly Run (MPS)
Months	6	18
Weeks	24	12
Days	14	

Two planning books: MPS, Standard

CTM Daily Run

Time Buckets pfl ID SNP Daily Time Bucket

Short text 1 Year Horizon: First 6 Months in Weeks: First 4 Weeks in Days

Number	Basic Periodicity	FYV 2	Display Periodicity	FYV 1
12			M	
6	M		W	
2	W		T	

CTM Weekly Run

Time Buckets pfl ID SNP Time Bucket

Short text 2 Year Horizon: First 12 Months in Weeks: Second Year in Months

Number	Basic Periodicity	FYV 2	Display Periodicity	FYV 1
18			M	
3	M		W	

The next step is to convert the "plain English" version of what we want into the SAP Planning Bucket Profile setting.

*The first row defines the entire length of the time horizon. The following rows define the different sections of the horizon. You make entries in the columns Number (of periods) and Display periodicity (or period types). The content of the other columns is displayed automatically when you press Enter. To see exactly which buckets will be displayed, choose Period list. A Planning Buckets Profile contains the periodicities or a subset of the periodicities that you defined in the Storage Buckets Profile. In a Planning Buckets Profile, do not include a periodicity that is not in the Storage Buckets Profile. Use the Planning Bucket Profiles that you created to define the future planning horizon and the past horizon by entering them in a planning book: one for the future planning horizon and one for the past horizon. The system displays the horizons in interactive demand and supply planning, starting with the smallest time bucket and finishing with the largest time bucket. The future horizon starts with the smallest time bucket on the planning horizon start date, and works forward, finishing with the largest time bucket. The past horizon starts with the smallest time bucket the day before the start of the future horizon and works backward, finishing with the largest time bucket. — **SAP Help**

It is not necessary to use a single periodicity (period type). Multiple periodicities can be used in the creation of a Time Bucket Profile, and can be shown in the Planning Book.

The book, *Sales and Inventory Planning with SAP APO,* has an excellent description of the logic of this screen.

The time horizon comprises two years in the example shown. Of these two years, the first six months are shown in weeks. The first four weeks of the first month are shown in days. As we can see, the remaining eighteen months are shown in months. The first line defines the entire length of the time horizon. The following lines define the various sections of the horizon. You make entries in the columns Number and Display periodicity. The content of the other columns is displayed automatically as soon as you press Enter.

To match our Planning Bucket Profile spreadsheet on the previous page, we would create the following entries in APO. Planning Bucket Profiles can be created with the same periodicity, or with mixed periodicities. When periodicities or period types are mixed (days, weeks, months, years) the vast majority of cases is to create a "telescoping" planning book. A telescoping planning book is used so that planners see small planning buckets close to the present day, and successively larger planning buckets as the planning horizon reaches out into the future. This is the preferred way for planners to see a planning book. Note that this has nothing to do with the Storage Bucket Profile, except that the Storage Bucket Profile must be as small as the smallest planning bucket used in the Planning Bucket Profile. To continue our example, we have decided upon the following telescoping planning bucket profiles. One will begin with days, and the second for the MPS (master production schedule) run will begin with weeks.

Maintain Time Buckets Profile DP/SNP

| ⊞ Period list   ⑦ 🗑 |

| Time buckets prfl ID | SCM FOCUS WEEKLY CTM |
| Short text | Weekly CTM Run |

Time Buckets Prof. Details

Number	Basic periodicity	FYV 2	Display periodicity	FYV 1	⊞
18			M		
3	M		W	⟳	

If you want to see precisely what periods are displayed, click on the Period list button.

Maintain Time Buckets Profile DP/SNP

[Period list] (?) 🗑

| Time buckets prfl ID | SCM FOCUS DAILY CTM |
| Short text | Daily CTM Run |

Periods in Time Buckets Profile ⊠

Start date   09.09.2012
End Date   31.08.2013

Time Buckets Prof. Details

Number	Basic periodicity	FYV 2	Display periodicity
12			M
6	M		W
2	W		T

PerId	Frm	To	Wrkdy
W	04.02.2013	10.02.2013	7
W	11.02.2013	17.02.2013	7
W	18.02.2013	24.02.2013	7
W	25.02.2013	03.03.2013	7
M	04.03.2013	31.03.2013	28
M	01.04.2013	30.04.2013	30
M	01.05.2013	31.05.2013	31
M	01.06.2013	30.06.2013	30
M	01.07.2013	31.07.2013	31
M	01.08.2013	31.08.2013	31

✓

While the configuration is counterintuitive, think of the process as moving from less detail to more detail.

A frequent request I hear from clients is for the ability to show planning periods that will happen in the near future in weekly planning buckets, with monthly planning buckets after this time period. Most companies would like to see their data in this manner, and doing so would reduce the computation performed by SCM (i.e., not having to calculate weekly buckets out for the entire horizon). The creation of a telescoping Time Bucket Profile is a frequent request on projects.

http://www.scmfocus.com/sapplanning/2010/02/24/the-storage-buckets-profile-and-the-planning-buckets-profile/

http://www.scmfocus.com/sapplanning/2011/02/22/why-supply-planning-order-batching-in-weekly-buckets-is-unnecessary/

The Time Bucket Profile is then assigned to the Planning Area.

Initializing Planning Area

Planning Areas are the central data structure for both DP and SNP, and they hold the key figures that are used in many places, but are shown prominently in the various DP and SNP Planning Books. Similar to the Storage Bucket and Planning Bucket Profiles, the Planning Areas must be initialized for both DP and SNP, and this transaction has a "from date" and "to date" as is described below:

More on Planning Areas is provided in this article:

http://www.scmfocus.com/sapplanning/2010/07/01/planning-areas/

The time objects described thus far are shown in the graphic below:

Major Time Related Objects in DP and SNP

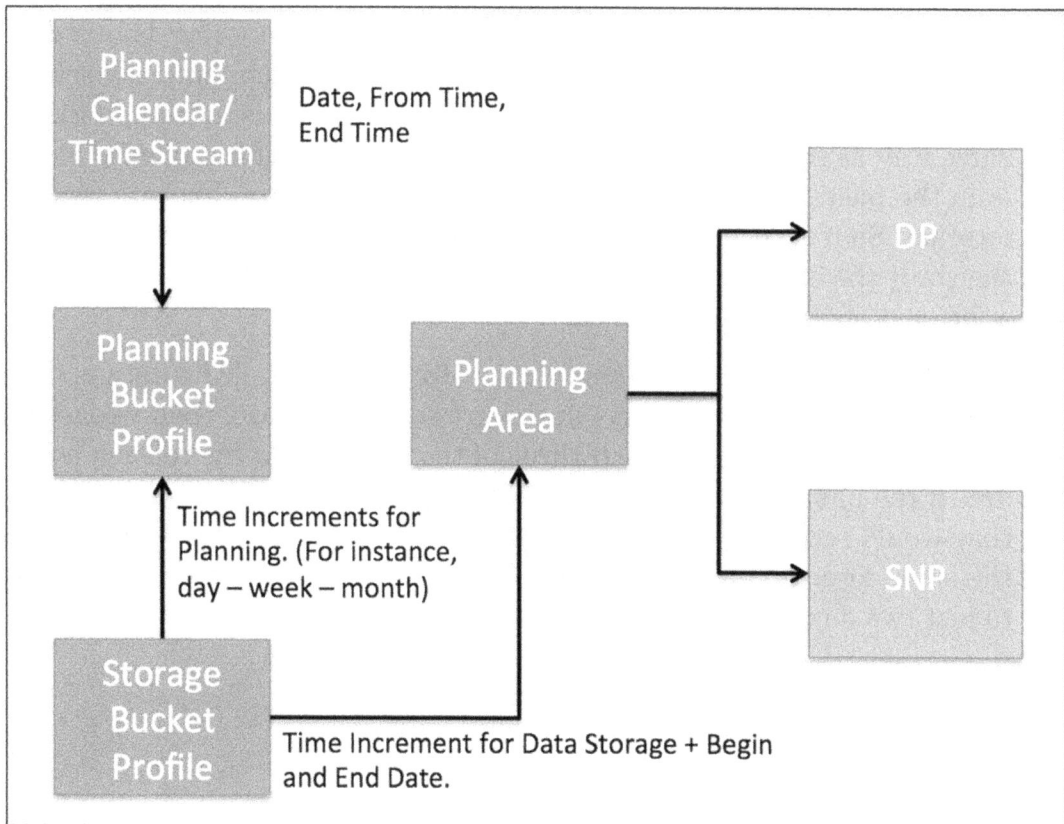

DP Period Split

The DP Period Split controls how the forecast—which is almost always in weekly storage buckets—is time disaggregated when sent to SNP. The DP Period Split field has three options:

1. *Split According to Workdays (Entire Period):* if blank—The data is disaggregated and released to all of the workdays in the specified horizon. This concept is the easiest to understand: If there is a forecast for 500 units for a week and the release horizon includes five workdays, each day would get a forecast of 100 units.

2. *Split According to Workdays (Proportional Period):* if 1—The data is disaggregated to all of the workdays in the specified horizon, but released only for those days that lie in the present and future. This setting works the same way as the previous setting, except when part of the release horizon is in the past. In this case, only the present and future buckets receive a forecast. So if three of the five days in the release horizon are in the past, then only the last two days would receive a forecast, and they would receive a forecast of 100 units per bucket.

3. *Split Entire Quantity Over Remaining Workdays:* if 2—The data is disaggregated only to the workdays in the present and future, then released for the same days. For example, if three of the five days in the release horizon are in the past, then only the last two days would receive a forecast, and they would receive a forecast of 250 units per bucket. They would receive the same forecast quantity as was in the week, but it would be allocated to just two days.

The screen shot below is an example of the DP Period Split Profile:

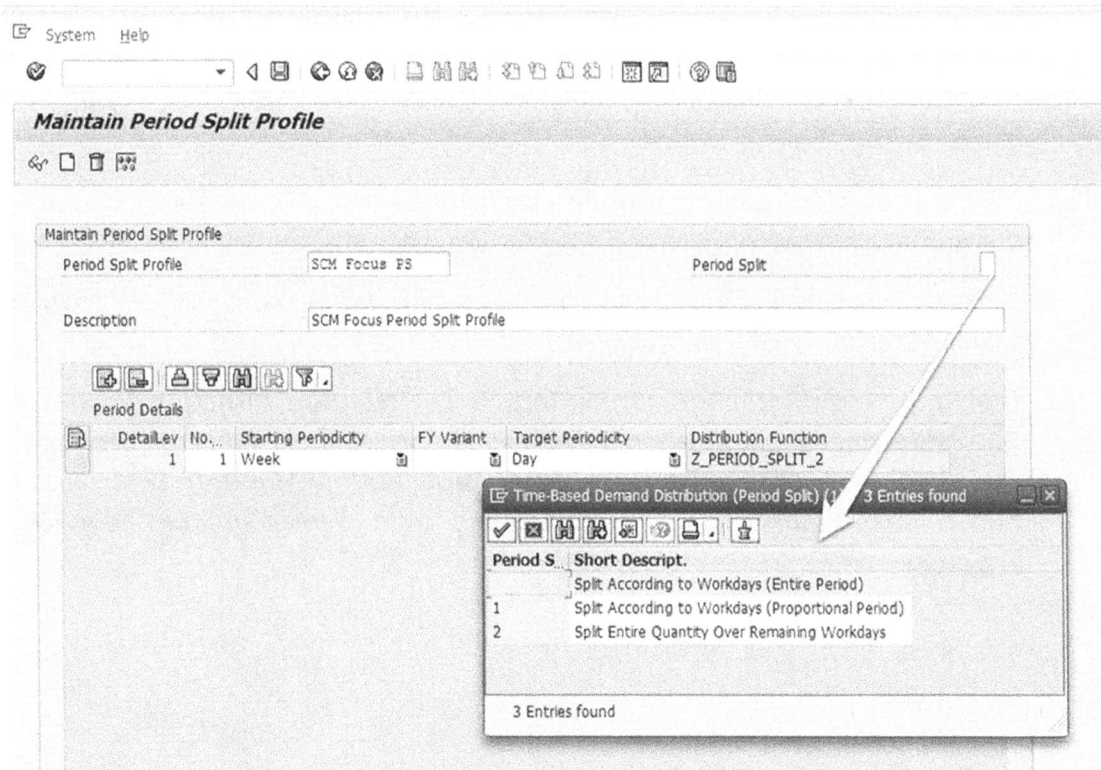

The Period Split field is defined both in (DP) Period Split Profile and also in the Product Location Master where it is part of the Demand Profile.

The forecast split can be adjusted per product-location combination, which is shown in Chapter 3: "SNP Horizons, Calendars and Timings." Both of these settings use the period split options, which are listed above. However, the period split is only one of the controls for how the forecast is distributed over the SNP periods. The other fields are important as well; however, these values only exist on the Period Split Profile, and not on the Product Location Master, which only holds the Period Split field.

The (DP) Period Split Profile has the following fields:

1. *Number of Periods: The number of periods for which the forecast release will be applied. Applies to the next field, "Starting Periodicity."*

2. *Starting Periodicity: The periodicity in DP (can be Weeks, Months, Quarters, Years, or the Posting Period).*

3. *FY Variant: Contains the number of posting periods in the fiscal year and the number of special periods.*

4. *Target Periodicity: The periodicity to release the forecast to SNP (can be Days, Months, Weeks, or Quarters).*

5. *Distribution Function: This points to a Distribution Function Profile. It causes the forecast to be distributed over the selected period very specifically and to a preprogrammed value, which is stored in the Maintain Distribution Function configuration transaction shown in the screen shot on the following page:*

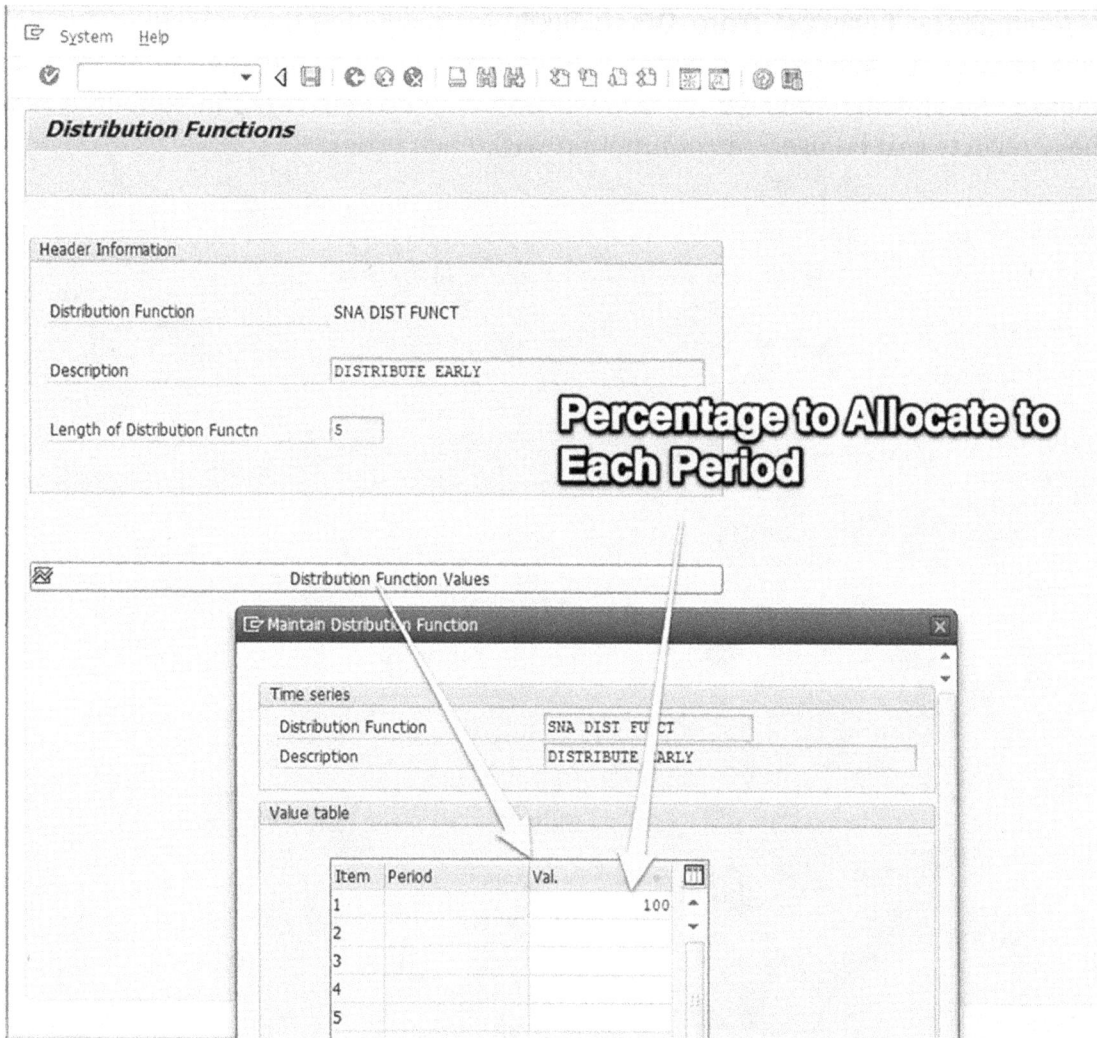

Here I have created a Distribution Function that applies the entire forecast to the first bucket—which if you check the DP Period Split Profile above, you will note is a day. This means that the weekly forecast—which is a weekly periodicity in the Period Split Profile—will be released/applied to the first day of the of the Target System. As long as the forecast is released before Tuesday, the weekly forecast from DP will be released/ applied to Monday.

Releasing the Forecast from DP to SNP

Now that we have defined a number of objects, we will use several of them to release the forecast from DP to SNP. Doing this exercise should reinforce how these objects can be used in conjunction with each other.

1. *Planning Area: We will want to release to the main Planning Area that we have been using.*

2. *Planning Version (Data Source): We will want to release from the active version. However, we may also create simulation forecasts or other non-live forecasts. If we wanted to release the simulation forecast we would change this number to 001, 002, etc., or whatever number has been assigned to the non-live forecast.*

3. *Key Figure (Data Source): The Key Figure that is to be released in DP. Because we are releasing the forecast Key Figure in DP, we will choose 9AAFCST.*

4. *Planning Version (Data Target): We want to release to the active version.*

5. *Category (Data Target): We will want to release to the Forecast category, which is FC. If we do this, the DP will appear in the Forecast Key Figure at the top of the 9ASNP94 Interactive Supply Network Planning Book, which is the final forecast. An example this forecast can be seen below:*

SNP PLAN	Unit	09.10.20	10.10.20	11.10.20	12.10.20	13.10.20	14.10.20
Forecast	EA	123	1,243	1,245			1,254
Original Forecast from Demand Plan	EA						
Sales Order	EA						
Distribution Demand (Planned)	EA						
Distribution Demand (Confirmed)	EA						
Dependent Demand	EA						
Total Demand	EA	123	1,243	1,245			1,254
Distribution Receipt (Planned)	EA						
Distribution Receipt (Confirmed)	EA						
Production (Planned)	EA						
Production (Confirmed)	EA						
Total Receipts	EA						
Stock on Hand	EA						
Supply Shortage	EA	4,568	5,811	7,056	7,056	7,056	8,310
Safety Stock (Planned)	EA						
Safety Stock	EA						
Reorder Point	EA						
Target Days' Supply	D						
Target Stock Level	EA						
Days' Supply	D						

Selected Objects

Product	Type	Location	Prod. Descript.	Location description
DEMO03		FACT	Zinfandel	San Diego Factory
DEMO03		DC	Zinfandel	San Jose DC
DEMO03		RDC	Zinfandel	San Francisco RDC

Selection profile
SCM Focus User 1
CTM_ROP_1
CTM_ROP_2
CTM_ROP_3

Forecast Released from SAP DP

Planning Book/Data View Description

APO Location   2WIR   APO Product   DEMO03

6. *Horizon: The interval over which the forecast should be released. I have chosen one month.*

7. *Planning Buckets Profile: The time bucket in which the data is displayed in DP and SNP.*

8. *Daily Buckets Profile: This defines the days that the system uses to release the demand plan to SNP. This is an optional field. If a daily buckets profile is used, it must only contain days.*

9. *Period Split Profile: This is how the forecast will be split and distributed to the storage buckets in SNP. As I have selected the SCM Focus PS profile (along with the Distribution Profile I associated with this Period Split Profile), it will distribute 100 percent of the forecast to the first day—Monday of every week.*

10. *Product: The forecast split will be applied for the products White Wine to Red Wine.*

11. *Location: The forecast split will be applied for the locations from San Diego to San Jose.*

All the settings can be saved as a variant so that the forecast release can be assigned to a Process Chain.

This is shown graphically below:

Release of DP Forecast to SNP

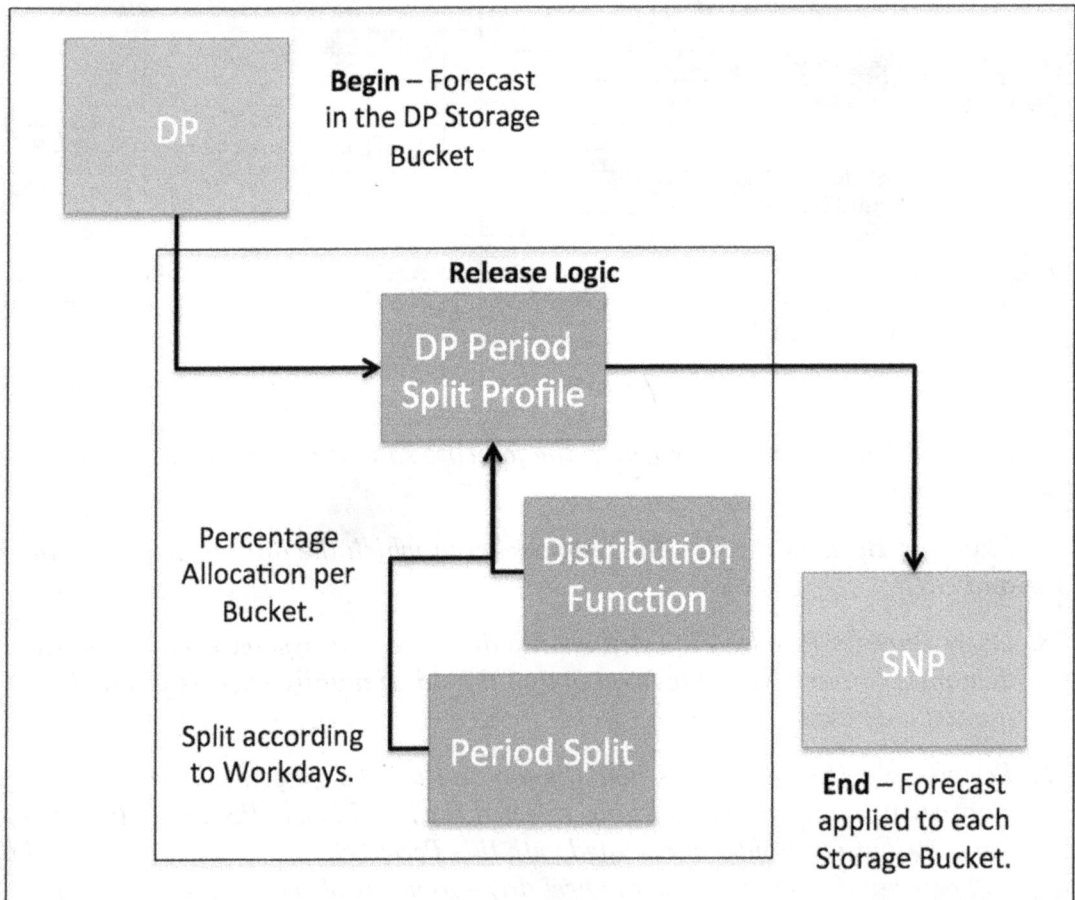

DP Planning Calendar/Time Stream

The planning calendar is created much like a profile, and then assigned to DP.

This is the header tab and contains the most basic information about the planning calendar.

1. *Years in the Past: This field controls how long in the past the DP Calendar will extend.*

2. *Years in the Future: This field controls how long out into the future the DP Calendar will extend.*

3. *Time Zone: DP requires that the UTC time zone be used.*

4. *Working Time Calendar (with Gaps): Includes holidays, days off, etc.*

5. *Period Calendar (without Gaps): Does not include holidays, days off, etc.*

6. *Calendar ID: This specifies non-working days.*

This is the calculation rule tab and it is where the working hours per day are defined:

1. From: Beginning of day.

2. To: End of the day

As defined above, this calendar has sixteen working hours set for each of the five working days.

This is the periods tab and simply takes the information from the first two tabs and declares the open period per the specific day. It also provides a field for comments, and allows the period to be fixed so that other automated changes cannot apply a new calculation to the period.

Demand Planning Frequency

In Chapter 8: "Critical Timing Topics," I cover the confusion between the planning and update frequency in multiple systems. I won't go into detail here, except to say that the most common demand planning frequency is weekly, with the provision for daily updates. The demand planning frequency is set in the Process Chain, which triggers the running of the forecast.

Conclusion

As with SNP, DP requires Storage Bucket Profiles and Planning Bucket Profiles. The Storage Bucket Profile controls how the planning data is stored and the Planning Bucket Profile controls how it is displayed in the Planning Books. The Storage Bucket Profile is assigned to the Planning Area, which is where the Key Figures central to the Planning Book are stored. The Storage Bucket Profile that is used by DP or SNP must always be in a periodicity that is smaller than or equal to the Planning Bucket Profile. Planning Bucket Profiles can be set up with a single periodicity (i.e. period type), but often have mixed periodicities or time intervals, which creates what is called a telescoping Planning Book. The Planning Bucket Profile can also have a Planning Calendar/Time Stream assigned to it. In this way, the Planning Bucket Profile can connect both the Storage Bucket Profile as well as the Planning Calendar/Time Stream. The Storage Bucket Profile is also assigned to the Planning Area.

To release the forecast from DP to SNP, it is necessary to set up a (DP) Period Split Profile. This profile, along with the Distribution Function (which is assigned to the Period Split Profile) controls how the forecast is allocated to the storage buckets in SNP. SAP allows great control over how the release of the forecast takes place with a wide number of fields—all of which were covered in the forecast release section of this chapter.

CHAPTER 3

SNP Planning Horizons, Calendars and Timings

Supply Planning Horizon Per Planning Run

Four types of planning runs are generally performed in any supply planning system.

1. *S&OP and Rough Cut Capacity Plan:* This is used for long-range planning and in most cases is an off-line analysis and is not part of the live environment.

2. *The Initial Supply Plan* (performed by MRP in ERP systems): Produces the initial production and procurement plan. It is focused on bringing stock into the supply network and on creating stock with planned production orders. Can also be called the master production schedule (MPS), if the initial supply plan is run under certain criteria. http://www.scmfocus.com/supplyplanning/2011/10/02/the-four-factors-that-make-up-the-master-production-schedule/

3. *The Deployment Plan* (performed by DRP in ERP systems): Focused on pushing stock from locations at the beginning of the supply network to the end of the supply network.

4. *The Redeployment Plan* (performed by specialized applications with redeployment functionality or with a custom report): Focused on repositioning stock, which is already in the supply network, to locations where it has a higher probability of consumption.

http://www.scmfocus.com/inventoryoptimizationmultiechelon/2011/10/redeployment/

Each planning run has a different planning horizon. I have listed the typical planning horizons below:

1. *S&OP and Rough Cut Capacity Plan:* A year or greater

2. *The Initial Supply Plan:* Most often a year

3. *The Deployment Plan:* Typically a few weeks

4. *The Redeployment Plan:* Typically three to six months

The S&OP planning run, Rough Cut Capacity Plan, and initial supply planning run all use the same three methods available in SNP that create planned production orders and create procurement recommendations to bring inventory into the supply network. These three methods are:

1. CTM

2. The SNP Heuristic

3. The SNP Optimizer

Deployment is accomplished with either the SNP ***Deployment*** Heuristic or the SNP ***Deployment*** Optimizer. My editor found this confusing, so let's list the different methods available for supply planning in SNP. There are two for the initial supply plan and one for deployment.

Initial Supply Plan/S&OP/Rough Cut Capacity Plan

1. CTM

2. The SNP Heuristic

3. The SNP Optimizer

Deployment

1. The SNP Deployment Heuristic

2. The SNP Deployment Optimizer

While the same methods may be used for each planning run, differences in the saved profiles or variants, including but not limited to the planning horizon (as well as different planning runs being performed in different versions—active, inactive etc.) provide the necessary planning output to meet the needs of each of the planning runs.

Redeployment is not a functionality that is covered by SNP, so I will not cover it in this book. For those who are curious as to whether one of the supply planning methods can be adopted to plan redeployment, after extensive testing and checking on this topic, I can say confidently that they cannot. For those wishing to integrate redeployment stock transport requisitions from outside of APO and incorporate them into APO, I cover this topic in detail in the book, *Multi Method Supply Planning in SAP APO*.

Supply Planning Horizon for S&OP, the Rough Cut Capacity Plan and the Initial Supply Plan

I will start by showing how the planning horizon is set for the SNP Heuristic, CTM and the SNP Optimizer, and then I will move to the topic of the SNP Deployment Heuristic and SNP Deployment Optimizer. In several areas I will refer to the "time stream," which is the official SAP terminology. A time stream applied to a supply planning method is usually that method's planning horizon.

SNP Heuristic Time Stream

On the screen shot on the following page you can see how the planning horizon is set with the SNP Heuristic.

Supply Network Planning: Planning Run

Display Logs

Data Source

Planning Book	9ASNP94
Data View	SNP94(1)
Global SNP Settings Profile	SAP
Paral. Proc. Profile	

- ⦿ Entire Planning Horizon
- ◯ Planning Horizon in Days   0

Object Selection

- ◯ Selection Profile
    - Selection Profile
- ⦿ Manual Selection
    - Planning Version

Product Number		to	
Location		to	
Low-Level Code		to	

Scope of Planning

- ⦿ Network (Heuristic)
- ◯ Location (Heuristic)
- ☑ Take into account found components in planning run
- ☑ Add products from supersession chains
- ☐ Net Change Planning

Source Determination	All Levels
Temporary Low-Level Codes	Do not use temporary low-level codes

On the SNP heuristic setup screen, a SNP Heuristic Profile can be set to process for up to the entire planning horizon (as set in the Planning Bucket Profile). In that case, one would make the setting the entire planning horizon option. If one wants to run the SNP heuristic for a time horizon shorter than the Planning

Bucket Profile (see the Planning Bucket Profile—or time stream for more details) then the second selection would state the planning horizon in days.

CTM Time Stream

The planning periods are additive and determine the planning horizon of CTM. In the screen shot below, I have created a CTM Time Steam that is made up of the following combination of periods. This time stream will begin with 14 days and then move to 10 periods of two weeks for twenty weeks.

Start

- ○ Fixed Start Date
- ◉ Relative Start   Days

☐ Start from Day of Week   0

Define Planning Periods

(1) Period Type   1   Days
No. of Periods   14

(2) Period Type   2   Weeks
No. of Periods   10

(3) Period Type
No. of Periods

(4) Period Type
No. of Periods

The time stream can be effectively shown in a spreadsheet, which also allows us to show multiple time stream settings close to each other. This is important, because a procedure will often have multiple runs and multiple time streams. In the example on the following page, we have one CTM Time Stream for a daily CTM run. The weekly run is for the long-range run, which is used in a company's S&OP process and master production schedule. This is shown in the screen shot below:

General Settings

Period	Daily Run	Weekly Run
Months	8	12
Weeks	22	52
Days	28	
Total in Months	14	24

CTM Time Stream

	CTM Daily	CTM Weekly
Description	CTM Time Stream for Daily Run	CTM Time Stream for Weekly Run
Fixed Start Date		
Relative Start Date		
Start from Day of Week		
Period Type	D	W
No. of Periods	28	52
Period Type	W	M
No. of Periods	22	12
Period Type	M	
No. of Periods	8	
Period Type	M	
No. of Periods	8	
Start Date		
End Date		

The mini spreadsheet at the top is the simplest way to state the periods and the number of periods. For the daily CTM run, the total time horizon that CTM will process is fourteen months, and the weekly CTM run is twenty-four months or two years.

Cost Optimization Time Stream

The cost optimizer in SNP is used for both what is referred to as the SNP Optimizer, which is also known as the SNP "network" Optimizer and is used for the initial supply planning run. The same cost optimizer is also used for the SNP Deployment Optimizer. So when I refer to "the SNP Optimizer," I am referring to the network optimizer which creates purchase requisitions and planned (production) orders. This is as opposed to the SNP Deployment Optimizer. This is not the clearest nomenclature I know, but it is the official nomenclature that SAP chose to use.

Both the SNP Optimizer and the SNP Deployment Optimizer are set up as profiles. This allows different variants or different settings for both optimizers to be saved and re-run in the future, and also for the variants to be scheduled. The optimizer profiles are broken into tabs, and I have only included the tabs, which have timing settings.

SNP Optimization Profile Maintenance

Profile

		Method	
Opt. Prfl.	SAP_ALL	⦿ Linear Optimization	☐ Automatic Cost Generation
Description	ALL CONTRAINTS	○ Discrete Optimizatn	

| General Constraints | Discrete Constraints | Model Params | **Solution Methds** | Integration | Autom.. |

Stop Criteria

Maximum Runtime (in Minutes)	
Maximum Number of Improvements	0

Decomposition

☐ Time Decomposition
    Window Size   3 Buckets
☐ Product Decomposition
    Window Size   30 %
☐ Resource Decomposition
Priority Profile

Priority Decomposition

⦿ Cost-Based Prioritization
○ Strict Prioritization
Safety Stock Priority   Regard as demand forecast

First Solution

☐ Heuristic First Solution

Two time settings at the top of this tab are related to either how many times the optimizer should process or how long the optimizer should run. Optimizers must be capped because they will simply continue to run unless told when to stop (optimizers will also eventually stop when they reach the objective function—or the "optimal" solution—is reached). However, in most cases the optimizer must be stopped well before it meets its objective function. The complexity and processing time for supply chain optimization makes it impossible to finish in a time that fits within the available processing window.

The Solutions Methods tab in the SNP optimizer allows the use of time decomposition, which is the most common type of decomposition. Time decomposition divides the problem into segments, which the optimizer then processes separately. For instance, if the time decomposition is set to "3," then the defined planning horizon is segmented into three components (from recent to further out) and the nearest planning time segment is processed first. Optimization decomposition is one of the most important things to understand about optimization and is described in more detail in the article below:

http://www.scmfocus.com/sapplanning/2011/10/12/snp-optimizer-sub-problem-division-and-decomposition/

Profile		Method	
Opt. Prfl.	SAP_ALL	◉ Linear Optimization	☐ Automatic Cost Generation
Description	ALL CONTRAINTS	○ Discrete Optimizatn	

General Constraints | Discrete Constraints | Model Params | Solution Methds | **Integration** | Autom...

Horizons
- ☑ SNP Production Horizon
- ☑ SNP Stock Transfer Horizon
- ☐ Forecast Horizon

Incremental Optimization

Dependent Demand for Fixed Orders	Regard as a hard constraint
Distribution Demand for Fixed Orders	Regard as a hard constraint
Substitution Demand for Fixed Orders	Regard as a hard constraint
Stock of Non-Selected PPM/PDS Input Products	Ignore
Stock of not Selected Source Location Products	Ignore

Setup Status Handling
- ☐ Cross-Period Lot Size Planning
- ☐ Lot Size Planning: Not Cross-Period

Existing Orders
- ☐ Do not delete any orders

Three timing settings on this tab simply tell the optimizer if they should use the SNP Production Horizon, the SNP Stock Transfer Horizon and the Forecast Horizon that are the Product Location masters. I discuss each of these horizons so I won't cover them here. The most important thing to understand is that specific runs of the optimizer can be made to simply ignore these values.

The Deployment Planning Thread

In SNP, confirmed STRs are only created by the deployment planning run. The deployment planning run follows the initial planning run and moves stock through the supply network. Deployment uses the initial supply plan to determine the plan for moving projected stock on hand through the supply network. The Deployment Plan (performed by DRP in ERP systems) is explained in the article below:

  http://www.scmfocus.com/sapplanning/2009/07/30/deployment-explained/

Now we will get into the various horizons of the deployment planning run.

The Deployment Heuristic

As with the initial supply planning methods, planning horizons are assigned to the deployment heuristic and the deployment optimizer profiles/variants.

The deployment heuristic uses a deployment horizon, which is stated in days and is shown above.

The deployment heuristic has very few settings overall and just one time-related setting.

The Deployment Optimizer

The SNP Deployment Optimizer is very similar to the SNP Optimizer with two important differences:

1. It does not include any settings for production, that is, it does not read PPM/PDSs, and does not offer discrete optimization options for production parameters.

2. Has a special tab for deployment parameters that the SNP Optimizer does not have.

Notice there are no production settings on the discrete optimization tab.

The SNP Deployment Optimizer gives you the option of setting the Pull Deployment Horizon, the Push Deployment Horizon and the SNP Checking Horizon in either the Product Location Master or in the SNP Deployment Optimizer Profile as is shown above. If nothing is entered in the SNP Deployment Optimizer Profile, the settings in the Product Location Master are used by the optimizer.

As with the SNP Optimizer, the SNP Deployment Optimizer can be run in the background and can have its planning horizon defined in a variant. This variant can be scheduled and run automatically and repetitively.

Other Deployment Time Settings

These deployment settings are on the SNP 2 tab of the Product Location Master, which I will cover in detail in the following section. These deployment timing fields are described below:

1. *Indicator—Real-Time Deployment: When activated, the deployment is based upon the most up-to-date planning results from the initial supply plan. This is used for fair share distributions. However, the real time deployment does not take into account quota arrangements or even the transportation lanes*

and any location other than the source specified. Therefore, stock transfers are only created between the deployment source location and the destination location.

2. *Distribution: Where you state if you want push, pull, or push/pull distribution. With push distribution, deployment pushes out all stock within the planning horizon. With pull distribution, nothing is distributed to the demand location prior to the need date. With push/pull distribution, material is moved immediately as with push—but for the pull horizon.*

3. *SNP—Checking Horizon in Days: This is an optional setting. It is used in deployment, both in the SNP Deployment Optimizer and in the Deployment Heuristic. This setting controls how the available-to-deploy quantity (ATD) is calculated. When enabled, the ATD for the push deployment horizon is reduced. It is a signal for the system to add the ATD receipts for the current period and the past period and remove all ATD issues within the checking horizon. When not specified, the system adds ATD receipts of the current and past periods and removes ATD issues for the periods.*

4. *SNP Stock Transfer Horizon (on the SNP 2 tab of the Product Location Master): The SNP Stock Transfer Horizon controls both when the unconfirmed STRs are generated (they are created during the initial supply plan and transfer distribution demand through the supply network) and when the confirmed stock transfer requisitions are created (they are generated by deployment). The question of an unconfirmed versus a confirmed STR can be a point of confusion. Why would anyone need an "unconfirmed" STR? The reason for this is that SNP needs a method of creating distribution demand and distribution receipts in a supply network. SAP could have named this object a number of things, but settled on "unconfirmed" STR. A confirmed STR is the result of a deployment run (either the deployment optimizer or the deployment heuristic). The SNP Stock Transfer Horizon control is helpful in essentially disabling SNP over a particular duration. I have used it in the past when Kanban is configured in SAP ERP to handle stock movements that are in the short term (say fourteen days out), with SNP taking over the planning after fourteen days. However, generally speaking, this setting is not used that frequently.*

The SNP stock transfer horizon and its relationship to the SNP Planning Horizon is described in the graphic below:

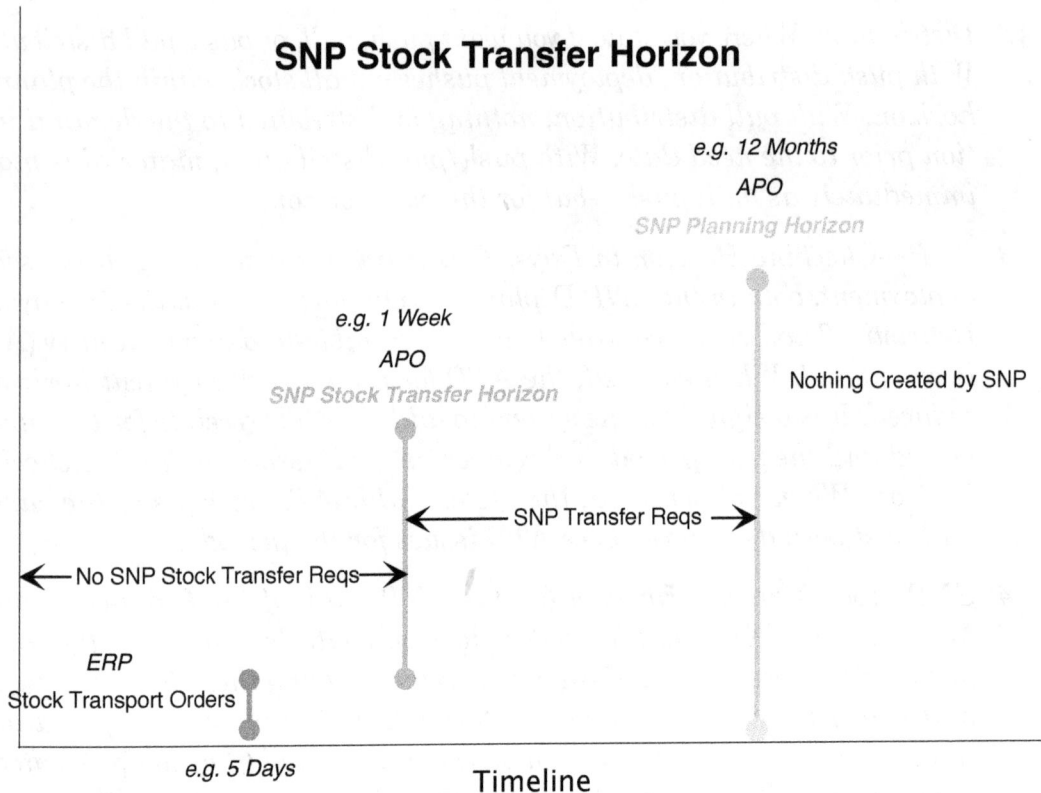

SNP Stock Transfer Horizon

e.g. 12 Months
APO
SNP Planning Horizon

e.g. 1 Week
APO
SNP Stock Transfer Horizon

Nothing Created by SNP

←――― SNP Transfer Reqs ――→

←― No SNP Stock Transfer Reqs―→

ERP
Stock Transport Orders

e.g. 5 Days   Timeline

Understanding the Time Settings and Profiles on the SNP 2 Tab

All of the supply planning methods use the fields that are on the Product Location Master, and the most fields are on the SNP 2 tab. While this is a well-known tab, the more one analyzes the time settings on this tab, the less logical the organization of the fields within the various areas of the tab appears. There are three profiles on the SNP 2 tab, as follows:

1. SNP Demand Profile

2. SNP Supply Profile

3. SNP Deployment Profile

The profile is an important way of controlling master data. A master data profile is simply a collection of master data fields, which are related and can be saved as a group or variant.

Of all the modules in APO, SNP has the most master data fields which may explain why SAP development was so liberal in their application of the profile concept to SNP master data fields. For instance, when a profile is saved in the SNP Demand Profile, the user has the option of filling in five other fields. Whenever this SNP Demand Profile is applied to a product-location combination, all of the applicable fields in the product location are populated at once. The fields for each of the profiles on the SNP 2 tab are shown on the following page:

Field	Profile?	Field Related To?
Demand Profile	Demand	Profile Name
Forecast Horizon	Demand	Forecast
Pull Deployment Horizon	Demand	Deployment
Period Split	Demand	Forecast
VMI Promo.L Time	Demand	Lead Time
Forecast Horizon in Past	Demand	Forecast
Supply Profile	Supply	Profile Name
SNP Production Horizon	Supply	Production
Extended SNP Production Horizon	Supply	Production
SNP Stock Transfer Horizon	Supply	STR Control
Push Deployment Horizon	Supply	Deployment
Deployment Safety Stock Push Horizon	Supply	Deployment
Fix Production	Supply	Production
Fix Stock Transfers	Supply	STR Control
Deployment Profile	Deployment	Profile Name
Push Distribution	Deployment	Deployment
Fair Share Rule	Deployment	Deployment
Consider Sales Order	Deployment	Deployment
Consider Forecast	Deployment	Deployment

Even though on this screen each field is assigned to a specific profile, the profiles are simply a way of grouping the fields. The fields can be grouped under other categories (such as function or purpose). If the same list above is sorted by what the field does, or what it is related to, the list looks like the following:

Field	Profile?	Field Related To?	Category
SNP Stock Transfer Horizon	Supply	STR Control	1
Fix Stock Transfers	Supply		
Demand Profile	Demand	Profile Name	NA
Supply Profile	Supply		
Deployment Profile	Deployment		
SNP Production Horizon	Supply	Production	2
Extended SNP Production Horizon	Supply		
Fix Production	Supply		
VMI Promo.L Time	Demand	Lead Time	3
Forecast Horizon	Demand	Forecast	4
Period Split	Demand		
Forecast Horizon in Past	Demand		
Pull Deployment Horizon	Demand	Deployment	5
Push Deployment Horizon	Supply		
Deployment Safety Stock Push Horizon	Supply		
Push Distribution	Deployment		
Fair Share Rule	Deployment		
Consider Sales Order	Deployment		
Consider Forecast	Deployment		

I have placed the fields into five categories: STR control, production, lead time, forecast and deployment. I don't include the name of the profile as a category, as it merely serves to group the associated fields. If one looks at the profile column it should be apparent that different categories of fields (that is, from a functionality perspective), are somewhat mixed up among the three different master data profiles.

However, one shouldn't assume that all fields that control the timings for a particular functionality area, even within the SNP 2 tab, are in its named profile. Furthermore, there are fields (such as the SNP Checking Horizon) that should be—or at least could be—part of the SNP Deployment Profile, but are not. Rather than discussing the timing fields by their appearance in the user interface, I wanted to discuss them by functionality. Doing so meant drawing upon different fields from different profiles. Consider this when viewing screen shots included in this book as we discuss the different timing categories. Throughout the book, rather than repeatedly showing the SNP 2 tab, I will ask you to refer back to the following screen shot to get your bearings as to where the fields I am discussing are located.

Forecast-related Supply Planning Timings

Demand planning settings are covered in Chapter 2: "DP Horizons, Calendars and Timings," so none of the timings discussed in this section should be confused with those discussed in the second chapter. SNP requires its own timing settings for how to work with the forecast. The following fields on the Product Location Master control the timing settings.

There are three fields on the SNP 2 tab that control the use of the forecast by SNP.

- *Forecast Horizon: Horizon in calendar days during which the forecast is **not** considered as part of the total demand. Within this horizon, Supply Network Planning (SNP) does not take the forecast into account when calculating total demand. Outside of this horizon, the system calculates total demand using either the forecast or sales orders (whichever value is larger), and the other demands (dependent demand, distribution demand, planned demand, and confirmed demand).*

- *Period Split (the official field name being Time Based Demand Distribution [Period Split]): Defines how planning data is disaggregated by time when you release the demand plan from Demand Planning to Supply Network Planning. The options are: blank—The data is disaggregated and released to all of the workdays in the specified horizon; "1"—The data is disaggregated to all of the workdays in the specified horizon, but released only for those days that lie in the present and future; "2"—The data is disaggregated to the workdays in the present and future, and then released for the same days.*

- *Forecast Horizon in Past: If you do not specify a value for the forecast horizon or enter the value 0 and set this indicator, the consumption logic of the forecast horizon also applies for planning periods situated in the past (before today's date). This is a rather convoluted way (Yes, the first part of this definition is from SAP—can't you tell?) of saying that just as with the Forecast Horizon (in the Future), the Forecast Horizon in the Past controls if the forecast is included in the backward consumption. This is a strange setting because if one does not want to perform backward forecast consumption, then simply don't use forecast consumption. I am not sure why I would ever want or need to enable this field, and I can't recall seeing it used for any of my SNP clients.*

SNP Forecast Horizon

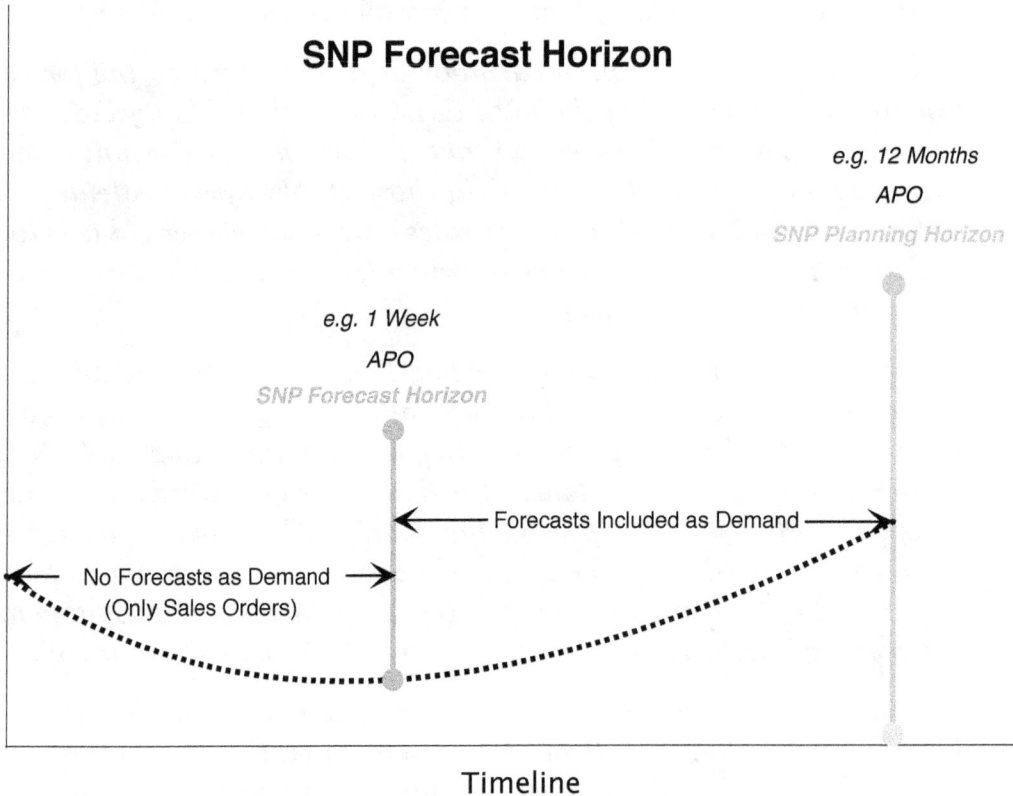

e.g. 12 Months

APO

SNP Planning Horizon

e.g. 1 Week

APO

SNP Forecast Horizon

← Forecasts Included as Demand →

← No Forecasts as Demand →
(Only Sales Orders)

Timeline

The SNP Forecast Horizon determines what is included as demand. The main use of this setting is to remove forecasts from the nearest period, the logic being that if the sales order has not materialized within, for example, the time period of one or two weeks out from the current day, it is unlikely that it will materialize at all (of course, this very much depends upon the situation, as many companies receive sales orders up to the current day). This setting prevents the company from building inventory that may not be consumed.

Because this setting is at a product location, the company can use it selectively for the product locations for which sales orders come in "x" number of days before the current day (where "x" is the duration of your choosing). I cover forecast consumption and the alternatives to it in Chapter 10: "Forecast Consumption, Allocation Consumption, Scheduling Directions and Timings."

Planning Calendars/Time Streams

This is a good point in the book to move to the topic of planning calendars/time streams. The planning calendar/time stream defines the following time information:

1. When the time stream begins (either a specific date, or a relative start date).

2. The length of the duration, in periods.

3. The different duration period types (days, weeks, months).

4. How many different duration period types will be in the time stream.

5. The sequence of the different duration period types.

Calendars/time streams in APO can be created in either the configuration area of APO or the SAP Easy Access menu with the transaction /SAPAPO/CALENDAR.

The planning calendar/time stream user interface is a bit unusual in that it can create a CTM time stream or a standard planning calendar/time stream. If a CTM time stream is selected, the options look quite a bit different than if the standard planning calendar/time stream is selected.

In this screen shot, we create a time stream/calendar for production. The options listed above are used to set up the CTM time stream. The way in which the time stream sequence is built is described in the post below (the CTM coverage is toward the bottom of the article):

http://www.scmfocus.com/sapplanning/2010/02/24/the-storage-buckets-profile-and-the-planning-buckets-profile/

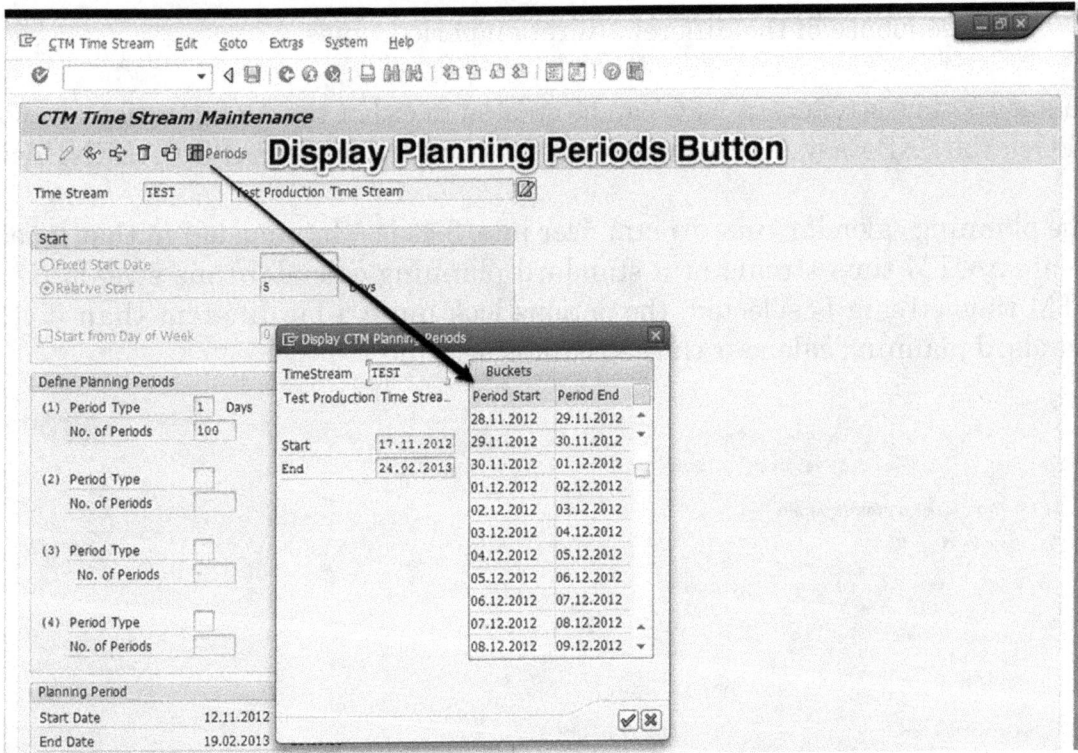

This screen serves as a quality check to ensure that the right periods are created. Within Time Stream Maintenance, one can select the Display Planning Periods button, which is useful because the time stream maintenance transaction is not particularly user friendly.

When creating a standard planning calendar rather than a CTM time steam, the following options are available:

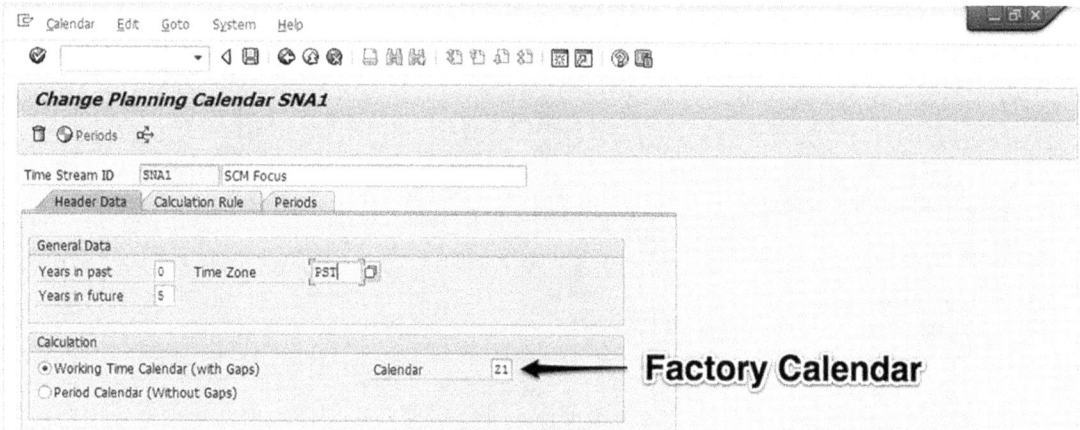

On this screen I can name the calendar, define how far into the future I would like the calendar to be valid, give it a time zone, state whether it is a working time calendar or a period calendar, and the assign a factory calendar to it.

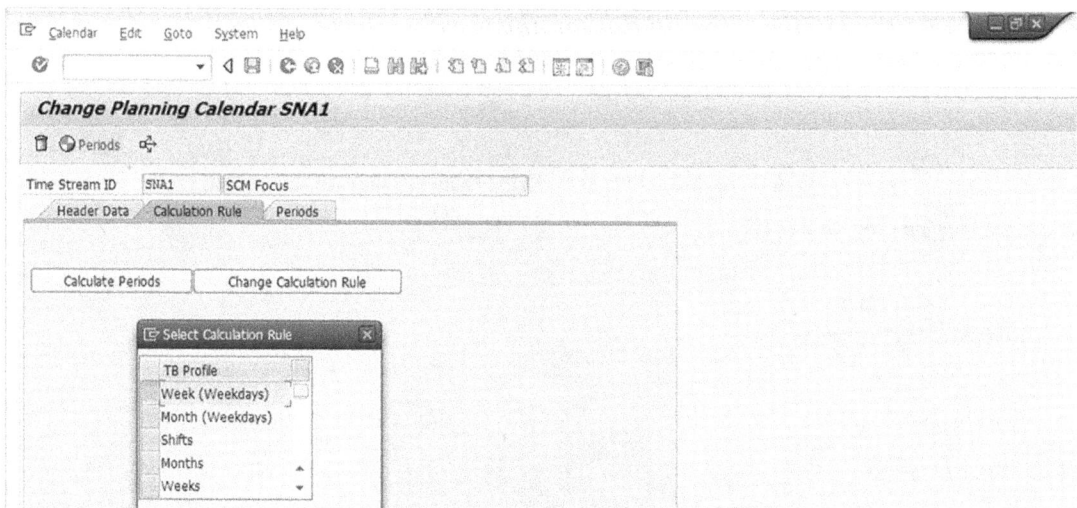

On the second tab I have to define a calculation rule, which chooses the periodicity of the calendar.

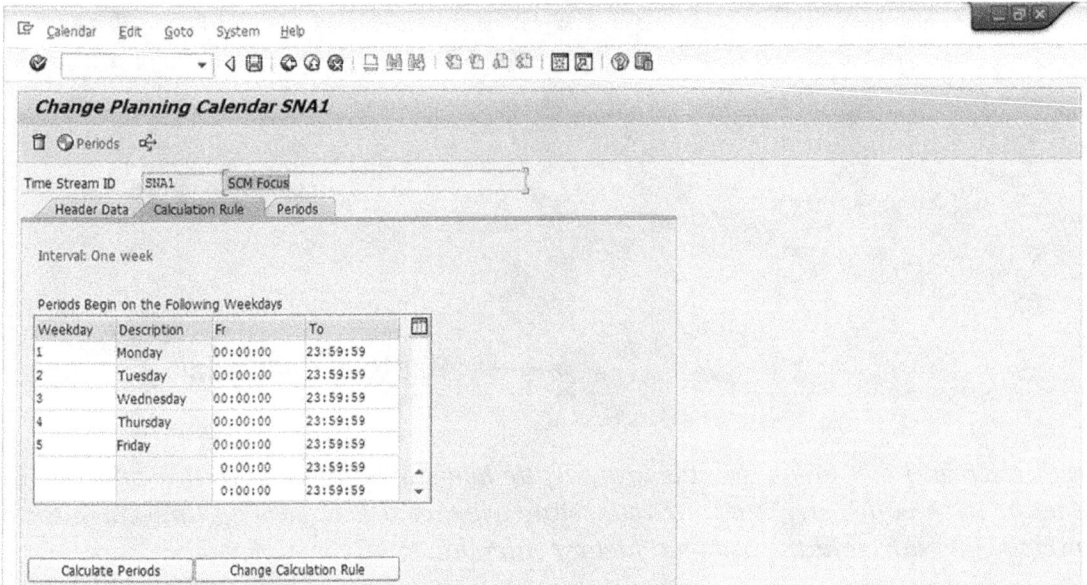

Here we can see the number of valid days in the weekly interval (selected on the previous screen). The number of valid days is inherited from the assigned factory calendar.

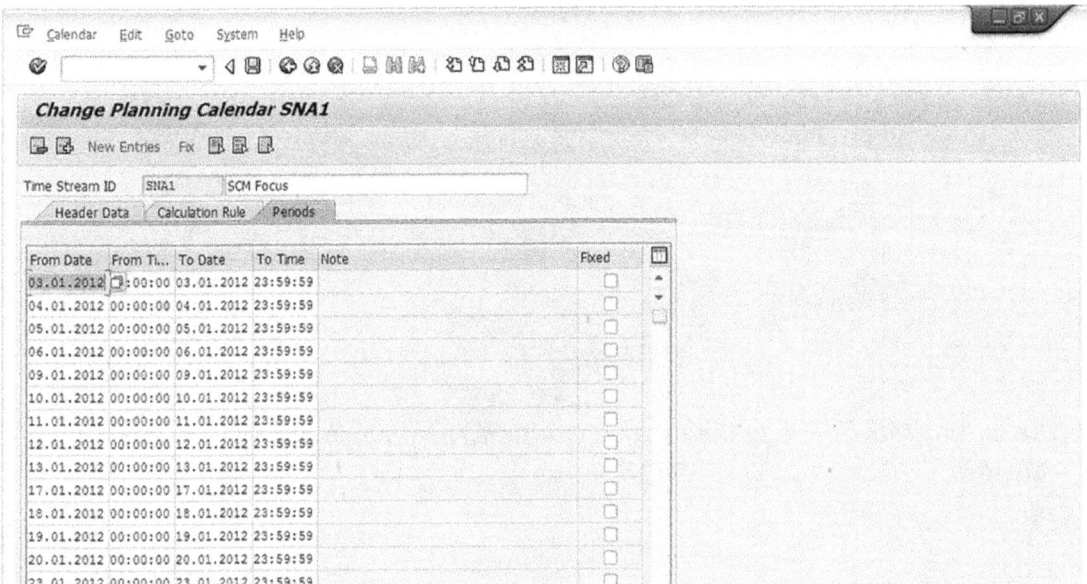

The third tab shows all of the specific valid time periods that have been created from the previous tabs.

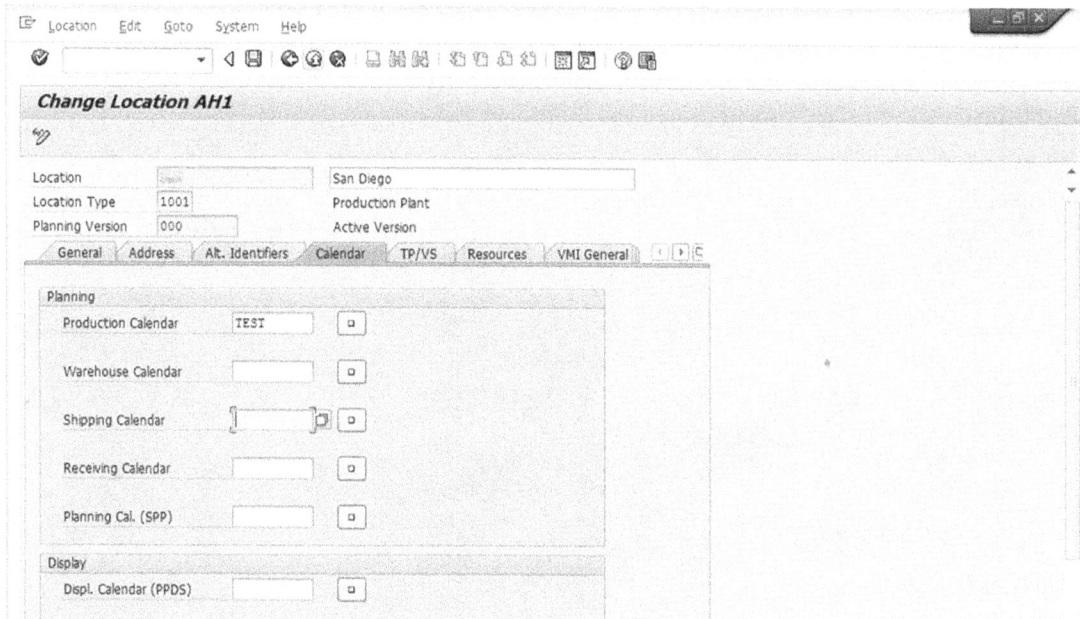

Now we assign the time stream to the location, which controls the timing for the location. There are six different calendars that can be associated with a location. These calendars control different aspects of the location's behavior.

The calendars tell SNP and PP/DS which days are available for planning in the factories and the distribution centers. The location calendar is the parent object, and then within the calendar, the resources are the children and they place a further constraint on capacity.

Supply Planning Timings Related to Lead Time

There are a variety of lead times in any supply planning system, but the most prominent are the lead times for procurement, production and stock transfer. While there are several important aspects to lead times, only one is focused upon: the actual duration that is entered as the lead time. The supply planning methods in SNP do not always consider the lead times that are entered as master data. How the lead times are treated depends very much upon the scheduling direction of the supply planning method used to plan the product location.

Each supply planning method can be scheduled either forward or backward. This is the scheduling direction setting for CTM. Constrained methods can use the backward or forward option. Unconstrained methods have the third and often default option, which is first backward and then forward.

When the scheduling direction is set to backward in the Product Location Master, the lead times control when activities are scheduled. When the scheduling direction is set to forward, lead times are not factored into scheduling and every demand is simply scheduled as soon as possible. This is covered in detail in Chapter 10: "Forecast Consumption, Allocation Consumption, Scheduling Directions and Timings."

Planning Delivery Time in Days

Planning delivery time is the lead time associated with ***external procurement,*** which is one of four options for the Procurement Type field on the Product Location Master. These options, which are listed below, can be set for any product-location combination.

1. External procurement

2. In-house planning

3. External or in-house production

4. External procurement planning

The Procurement Type is the basic setting for whether a product is produced internally, procured externally, or both. Production takes place in internal locations, and in most cases externally procured product will be produced by vendors/ suppliers that are not modeled as locations in SNP. When this is the case, the lead time is taken from the Procurement Tab of the Product Location Master. However, a vendor may also be set up as a location in APO. I cover the alternatives in this area in my book, *Setting up the Supply Planning Network in SAP APO*, so I will not cover that topic in this book.

The lead times are of course a major input into planning systems, as they determine when supply chain planning requisitions need to be created. In most cases the planning method is set to backward scheduling, which means that the calculation of dates for planned orders (which convert to either a production order or purchase order) and stock transfer requisitions is based upon subtracting the lead times from the need dates. SNP lead times include the following:

1. Inter and intra location lead times (which include procurement lead times and internal location-to-location lead times).

2. Non-production location processing times (goods issue, goods receipt)

3. Production lead times.

Transportation Lanes for Location-to-Location Lead Times

The lead times for all locations within the supply network (as well as vendor locations where it has been decided that their manufacturing capacity will be represented in SNP) are determined by the durations placed into transportation lanes.

But before we get into the time settings on the transportation lanes, it's important to explain a basic fact about them that tends not to be discussed in all of the written material on them, and that is that transportation lanes in APO are quite a handful in terms of the quantity of fields available and the complexity of the interactions of the different master date category types. Furthermore, transportation lanes take a while to get used to, because they are not simply the location-to-location routes that transportation lanes are generally thought of outside of APO. SAP development decided to make different categories of transportation master data and connect them together in a way that looks deceptively simple in the transportation lane configuration screens. In fact, the way that they developed the transportation master data is on its face confusing, and is a continual source of confusion on APO projects. In order to accommodate a wide variety of functionality, SAP created a distinct set of related transportation lane master data categories. In fact, of all the supply planning applications I have used since 1997, I have never seen one that came even close to the functionality and options available within APO's transportation lanes, and I would be surprised if another supply planning application exists that matches APO in transportation lane functionality, but also transportation lane confusion. In fact, this section of the book had to be rewritten several times because the inherent complexity of the transportation lane makes it not only difficult to understand but difficult to explain. SAP has put very little effort into explaining how the transportation lanes work, and the interrelationship between the different master data categories. They simply explain each of the transportation lane master data categories in isolation, and never attempt to connect the areas in a comprehensive fashion.

The transportation lane master data categories are listed below:

1. *Transportation Lane Header:* Holds the basic information about the transportation lane, most importantly its origin location and destination location. This is a mandatory category. All other master data categories are associated with a Transportation Lane Header.

2. *Product-specific Transportation Lane:* Transportation lanes can be defined per product, or they can be defined for all products. If one wanted a product-specific transportation lane to be valid for all products, one would create one entry in the Product-specific Transportation Lane for "all products."

3. *Means of Transport:* The mode of transportation (rail, truck, air, ship, etc.), as well as the equipment (20 foot container, 40 foot container, etc.) that is valid along the Transportation Lane source and destination location.

4. *Product-specific for Means of Transport:* These are the fields that are relevant for that means of transport for the specific product. This has few fields because this master data category primarily connects products with the means of transport.

5. *TSP (Transportation Service Provider) for Means of Transport:* These are the fields that are relevant for that means of transport for the specific product. This has the fewest fields of the three different transportation lane settings and, in fact, at many accounts is not even used. This category of master data is only used for the TP/VS module, which I don't cover in this book.

The following graphics provide a good jumping off point to understand transportation lanes and are important to review before we get into the fields that are assigned to each transportation lane master data category.

Transportation Lane Master Data Categories and Relationships

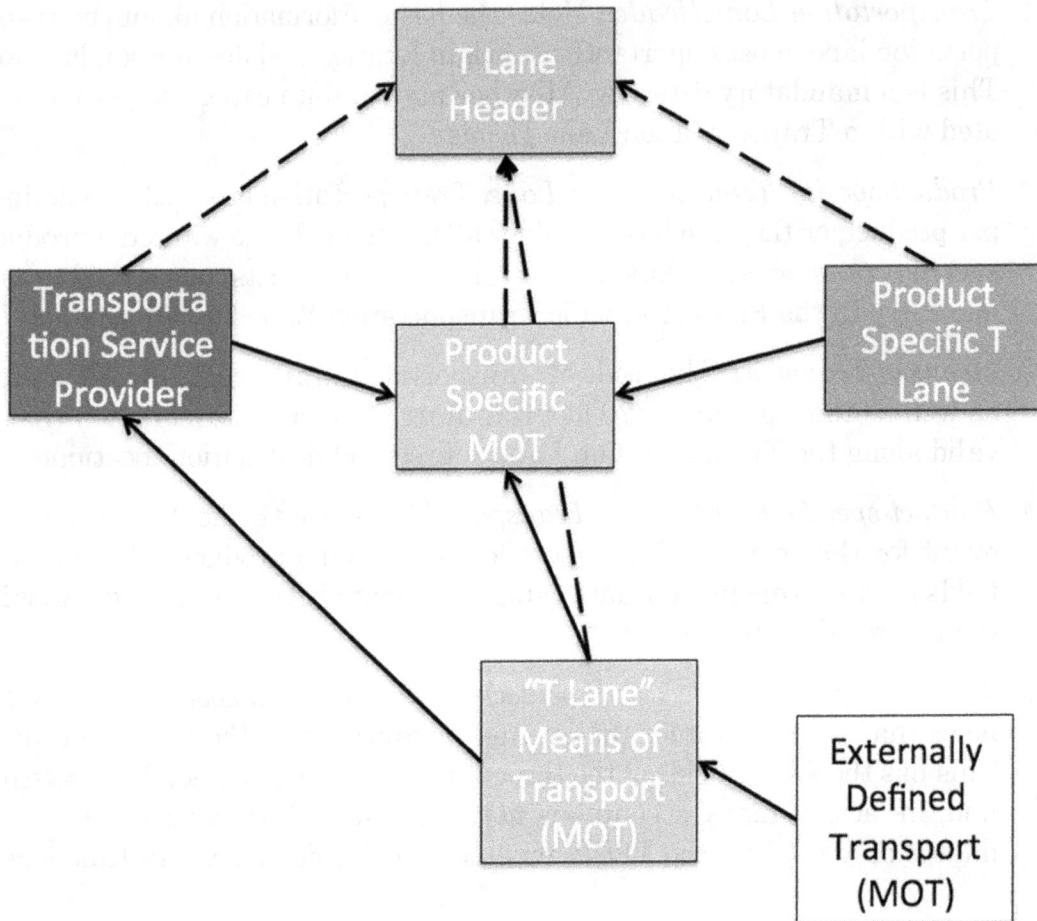

Here you can see the transportation lane master data categories that we will be covering. The dotted lines are meant to show the master data categories that are assigned to or owned by the Transportation Lane, which I refer to as the header to differentiate it from the other main master data categories. There are actually few fields contained in the header, and it is mainly an object that is used to assign the other more detailed master data categories or objects that do the actual heavy lifting.

The solid lines in the graphic on the previous page show how the master data categories are assigned to one another. For instance, the Product Specific Transportation Lane is object is assigned to the Product Specific MOT.

The very problematic part of the design of the transportation lane is evident from the bottom of the graphic. Within the transportation lane user interface/transaction, a MOT can be set up. However, this transportation lane MOT has another MOT that is assigned to it. This is what I refer to as the external MOT (although that is not what SAP calls it), which is defined outside of the transportation lane and is also called a MOT by SAP. I have called the transportation lane MOT the "TLane" MOT in the graphic on the previous page.

Also, notice in the graphic on the previous page that the externally defined MOT has no dotted line to the TLane header and it has a white background. This was done in order to differentiate it from the externally defined MOT. The following screen shot shows this external MOT configuration screen:

| Table View | Edit | Goto | Selection | Utilities(M) | System | Help |

Change View "Means of Transport": Overview

New Entries

Means of Transport

MTr	Std Code	Average Speed	Factor	Setup Time	Work.Time	Transport...	
0001	031	80,000			24:00	ROAD	
0002	072	100,000			24:00	RAIL	
0003	006	800,000			24:00	AIR	
0004		100,000			24:00	MAIL	
0005	011	30,000			24:00	SEA	
0006	038	60,000			24:00	ROAD	
SUBC	031	80,000			24:00	ROAD	

As you will see in the screen shots I will show later on, the external MOT is assigned to the TLane MOT. At first glance, it may appear that the external MOT simply populates the TLane MOT with its data. However, this is not correct, although a natural assumption to hold. Of the roughly eighty fields that make up the TLane MOT and the external MOT, the objects only share two fields, that being the name of the external MOT and its description. By using the nomenclature in this way, SAP guaranteed maximum confusion, as what we have are two completely different objects, which have the same name.

Transportation Lane Master Data Categories and Relationships and External Master Data Objects

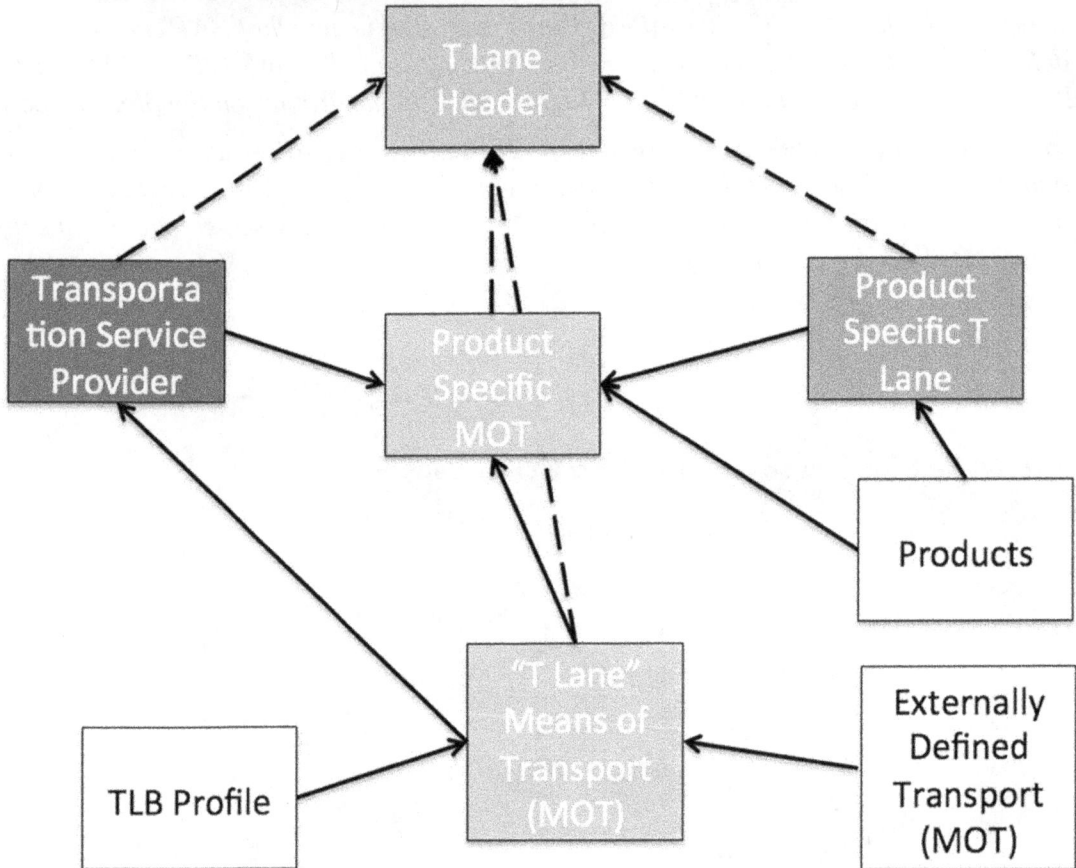

This graphic is an extension of the earlier graphic to show that the various transportation lane master data categories have a number of externally defined objects—some master data and some configuration, that can be selected to populate these master data categories. Of the roughly thirty fields that make up the TLane MOT—that are not inherited from the externally defined MOT, I counted nineteen which fall into this classification.

Outside of SAP, a transportation lane is often described as a transportation connection between two locations. This definition works well enough when discussing SNP some of the time, mostly when conversing at a high level. However, as can be seen on the previous page, there are actually multiple aspects or dimensions that SAP in one shape or form calls an aspect of a "transportation lane." All are important to understand and can be seen clearly in the transportation lane setup. Therefore, a "transportation lane" is all of the following:

1. A transportation relationship between two locations.

2. The product-specific transportation relationship between two locations.

3. A relationship between two locations for a particular means of transportation (truck type 1, truck type 2, rail, air, etc.) for all products, or a group or selection of products.

4. A relationship between two locations and a particular means of transportation (truck type 1, truck type 2, rail, air, etc.).

This can be seen in a matrix form below:

Transportation Lane Master Data Category	Relationships		
	Locations	Product	Means of Transport
Transportation Lane Header	X		
Product Specific Transportation Lane	X	X	
Means of Transport	X		X
Product Specific Means of Transport	X	X	X
Transportation Service Provider for MOT	X		X

Obviously, master data parameters that would apply to a product-specific transportation lane would not apply to a means of transportation.

In addition to all the confusing logical issues with the transportation lane, the transportation lane user interface is also tricky. Sometimes it takes several selections of certain header buttons to bring up the right screen, and a user can think they are in one view when in fact they are in another. For this reason, I have included a marked-up version of the transportation lane user interface.

The graphic on the following page explains where some of the important fields are located in the different transportation lane screens.

Transportation Lane Screens

Transportation Lane Dimension	Transportation Lane Header	Prod.Spec. Product Specific Transportation Lane	Means of Transport	Prod.Spec. Means of Transport Product Specific for Means of Transport	TSP for Means of Transport
Available or Blocked		X			
GR Processing Tme		X			
Loading Method			X		
Lot Sizes		X		X	
Maximum Distance					X
Priority		X			X
Pull-in Horizon			X		
Resource Assignment			X		
Stacking Factor				X	
TLB Profile			X		
Transp.Planner Assign.	X				
Transportation Calendar			X		
Transportation Costs			X		X
Transportation Distance			X		
Transportation Duration			X		
Type of TLane (Std, SubK, Consign)		X			

The graphic on the following page shows where the various dimensions of transportation lanes are located on the panes on the left side of the user interface.

Transportation Lane A to B

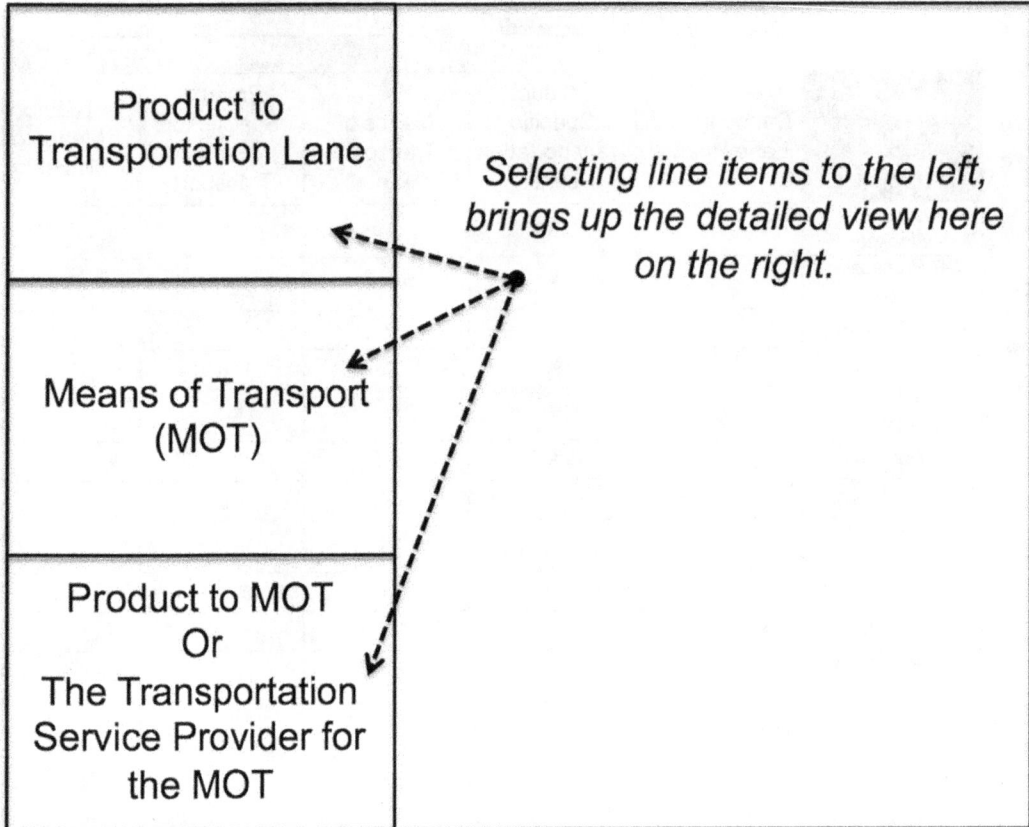

Product to
Transportation Lane

Selecting line items to the left,
brings up the detailed view here
on the right.

Means of Transport
(MOT)

Product to MOT
Or
The Transportation
Service Provider for
the MOT

Different lead times apply for different types of transportation lanes. Transportation lanes hold a large amount of information, including transportation costs and distance; however, for this book I focus on the time settings for transportation lanes.

If you want to learn more about transportation lanes—outside of their timings—
SCM Focus has several articles that can be found at the links below:

http://www.scmfocus.com/sapplanning/2011/09/23/transportation-lane-
settings/

http://www.scmfocus.com/sapplanning/2009/06/20/transportation-lanes-in-
scm/

http://www.scmfocus.com/sapplanning/2008/09/14/snp-transportation-lane-
and-transportation-resource-setup/

Transportation Lane Header

The header of the transportation lane is one of several views of the transportation
lane master data categories that can be arrived at by selecting one of the buttons
along the header of the transportation lane user interface.

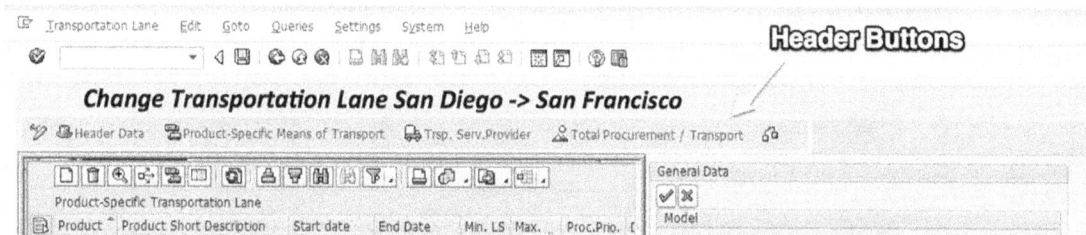

*If we select the Header Data button—located at the far left on the header bar—we will
be taken to the header data, which is called "General Data" in the interface.*

The header of the transportation lane contains basic information such as the model, the start and end locations, and the planner associated with the transportation lane. There are only two time-related fields for the header of the transportation lane.

1. *Order Processing Calendar: This field works like any of the other calendar/ time stream assignments.*

2. *Communication Duration: I can find no documentation on this field and have never seen the field used.*

3. *Correct Freeze Period: This field applies to the SPP module, and since I do not cover the SPP module in this book, I will not get into it.*

Product-Specific Transportation Lane

For some reason, when a transportation lane is selected in the left pane of the user interface, the term "Product Procurement" appears at the top of the right side of the user interface. This screen is, in fact, the Product Specific Transportation Lane. The right side of the user interface shows the same fields that are in the left side, but shows it in a more digestible format.

Time-related fields for the product-specific transportation lane include the following:

1. *Start Date: When the transportation lane becomes active.*

2. *End Date: When the transportation lane is to be deactivated.*

3. *GR Processing Time (Full field name = Consider Goods Receipt Processing Time):* *Controls whether the system should take into consideration for source determination the goods receipt processing time from the transportation lane. The system automatically adopts the goods receipt processing time in SAP ERP in the transportation lane during the Core Interface (CIF) transfer of scheduling agreements and contracts from SAP ERP. At the same time, the system also selects the GR Processing Time checkbox. If the checkbox is selected, the system explicitly uses the goods receipt processing time from the transportation lane for source determination. (This is normally applied at the product-location combination, but as you can see on the previous page, it can be applied to the product-specific transportation lane). When this is enabled, it overrides any value populated in the Product Location Master.*

4. *Consider GR Processing Time: Controls whether the system should take into consideration for source determination the goods receipt processing time from the transportation lane. The system automatically adopts the goods receipt processing time in SAP ERP in the transportation lane during the CIF transfer of scheduling agreements and contracts from SAP ERP. At the same time, the system also selects the GR Processing Time (Consider Goods Receipt Processing Time) checkbox. If the checkbox is selected, the system explicitly uses the goods receipt processing time from the transportation lane for source determination.*

5. *Planning Horizon: For the Transportation Load Builder—how far out the Transportation Load Builder (TLB) looks for Stock Transport Orders can be assigned in the TLB run, or in the transportation lane with this field.*

6. *Usage—Lead Time: Clears up the possible conflict between the system using the procurement lead time that is in the Product Location Master. Here you can tell APO which to use. The options are "Maintained Procurement Lead Time" or "Calculated Procurement Lead Time" (the second option uses the inputs to the Transportation Lead Time).*

7. *Horizon for Expected Receipts: The horizon for expected receipts at the sending location during deployment. Considers ASNs, STOs, and receipts from suppliers for DRP.*

Product-Specific Transportation Lane

Product	Prod.Desc.	Start date	End Date	Min. LS	Max. LS	Proc.Prio.	Dist.Prio.	Proc.Costs	Cost Fun
FG	FG	24.08.2012	31.12.9999	0,000	0,000	0,00	0,00	0,00	

Means of Transport

MTr	MTr Descr.	Start date	End Date	All Prods	Aggr. Plng	Detld Plng	Trsp. Cal.	Fix Duratn	Trsp. Du
0001	Truck	24.08.2012	31.12.9999	✓	✓	✓		□	

Product-Spec. Means of Transport For Product FG

Product Number	MTr	Start date	End Date	External Procurement Rel.	Not Allowd	Transptn Costs	Unit

Production Time [_____] Hours
Usage: Lead Time — Maintained Procurem...
Horizon for Expctd Receipts [ ] Days
Horiz. Fut. Aval. Whse Stck [ ] Days
ID Supplier Shutdown
Sync. Cal. for Goods Receipt
Dyn. freeze horizon
Order Type Inv.Bal.Unsrv. — Stock Tra...

Form of Procurement
⦿ Standard
○ Subcontracting
○ Consignment
Creation Indicator — Default

External Procurement Relationship
Source Category
Purchasing Doc. No.
Purchasing Doc. Item — 0
Purchasing Organiz.
Planned Deliv. Time

Sales Scheduling Agreement
Sales Document No.
Sales Document Item — 0
Sales Organization

8. *Synchronized Calendar for Start of the Goods Receipt: This is exactly what it says: a synchronization setting for the goods receipt of external orders.*

9. *Dynamic Freeze Horizon: This field is used by SPP, so I will not cover it.*

10. *Direct Delivery: This indicator is relevant to the heuristic in Supply Network Planning (SNP). It specifies that this transportation lane is considered by the SNP heuristic for direct deliveries from a production location to a customer location. Thus, there is no detour via a distribution center. The system first checks if product quantities can be delivered via flagged transportation lanes. Then the system covers any remaining quantities with the standard source determination.*

11. *Planned Delivery Time: The number of days needed for external procurement.*

Means of Transport Transportation Lane

The next set of timings is for the Means of Transport Transportation Lane.

1. *Start Date: When the means of transport is valid for use.*

2. *End Date: When the means of transport expires.*

3. *Fixed Transportation Duration: Indicates that the specified duration of transportation will not be overwritten by an automatic calculation of the durations of transportation.*

4. *Transportation Calendar: Declares when transportation activities can be scheduled. Works the same way as the location and resource calendars/time streams described previously.*

5. *Transportation Duration: The time required by the vehicle to transit between locations. Along with the transportation calendar, these are the most important time settings on the transportation lane.*

6. *Bucket Offset for Production Availability During Shipment: Tells the system if the delivered stock can be used at the start of this bucket or should be pushed to the next bucket (bucket being a day). For this purpose, the system uses two rounding limits:*

one for transported products and one for produced products. These rounding limits are used in the following way: First, the system evaluates the relevant calendars to determine the exact availability date of the products. Then, the length of the bucket based on this date is multiplied by the percentage specified in this field, to calculate the rounding limit within this bucket. The standard and recommended value is 1, which means that the production is available at the beginning of the bucket containing the stock transfer end date. Any value entered in the transportation lane overrides the value stored in the optimizer profile. This of course also means that the value in the optimizer profile can apply for a portion of the means of transport, but selective means of transport can have this value populated, giving them a different value per means of transport per transportation lane.

7. *Period Factor for Calculating Availability: You can enter a factor between **0** and **1**, where **0** is the start of the period, **0.5** the middle, and **1** the end of the period. When calculating the availability date/time, the system takes into consideration all weekdays, meaning that it does not take into consideration any days that have been defined as non-workdays in the calendars.*

8. *TLB Pull-In Horizon: The system looks for deployment stock transfers when it performs shipment upsizing. Therefore, this is how far out the transportation load builder (TLB) can look for STOs in order to upsize the order. This is an optional setting, as TLB does not necessarily have to do shipment upsizing. Whether it does or does not is controlled in the SNP Basic Settings under Make TLB Basic Settings.*

9. *Additional Stop Duration: The stop duration indicates the time that a means of transport is not in motion between two locations. It thus represents an addition to the duration of actual transportation. The duration of transportation represents the pure travelling time (working time, net transportation time), whereas the stop duration is defined as a gross time (that is, it relates to both the working time and the non-working time of the means of transport).*

Product Specific Means of Transport
The next set of timings is for the Product Specific Means of Transport.

1. *Selection: This is not a timing-related field, but shows that the Product Specific Means of Transport can apply for one product. There is also a selection drop-down, which allows many products to be added to the Product Specific Means of Transport, so this dimension of the transportation lane could also be called the Product(s) Specific Means of Transport. Alternatively, you can apply it to all products.*

2. *Valid From: The validity from-date of the selected products for the Means of Transport.*

3. *Valid To: The validity to-date of the selected products for the Means of Transport.*

4. *MOT Valid From: The validity from-date of the MOT (Means of Transport).*

5. *MOT Valid To: The validity to-date of the MOT.*

6. *Per: Allows a consumption to be stated in a time unit of measure for the transportation resource. However, it is extremely rare to set up transportation resources in SNP.*

Transportation Service Provider for Means of Transport

Transportation lanes are set up with the actual sending location of stock being the source location, and the receiving location being the destination.

Help

Serv.Provider   Total Procurement / Transport

Min. LS	Max.	Proc.Prio.	Dist.Pri	Prc
0,000	0,000	0,00	9,00	
0,000	0,000	0,00	1,00	
0,000	0,000	0,00	0,00	

Trsp. C	Fix Duratn	Trsp. D	Stop Dur.
TRANS	☐	48:00	

Costs	Unit	BUn	Transptn Cost

Transportation Service Provider

Trsp. Service Provider	SCM Focus Trucking

Validity

Means of Transport	Y1000
Start Date	01.03.2010
End Date	31.12.9999

Internal Costs

Transportation Costs		per	
	1.38	per	KM

Strategy

Priority	

Continuous Move

Arrival Window From	☐		Hours
Arrival Window To	☐		Hours
Depart. Window From	☐		Hours
Depart. Window To	☐		Hours
Maximum Distance			KM
Discount		15	

Share of Business

There are very few timing settings related to the Transportation Service Provider for Means of Transport. The timing settings are primarily related to the validity of the master data category.

1. *Start Date: Date from which the TSP (Transportation Service Provider) is valid.*

2. *End Date: Date when the TSP is no longer valid.*

3. *Arrival Window From: These four fields apply to continuous move. Enabling APO for continuous move makes SNP attempt to reduce the costs of shipment by assigning additional shipments to the TSP. APO allows for both simple continuous moves as well as round-trip continuous moves. As the functionality is used very rarely, I will not get into more detail on this topic.*

4. *Arrival Window To: The following three fields are the time limitations of the object.*

5. *Depart Window From:*

6. *Depart Window To:*

Padding the Time Prior to the Item Becoming Available

Often the transportation duration must be padded to account for any number of activities that lengthen out the time until the product should appear as planned stock-on-hand at the receiving location. Several of the timing fields can be used to "pad" the overall time as follows:

- *Transportation Duration: This is not a field that is actually designed to pad the transportation lane duration. The transportation duration should be the actual time it takes for the transportation activity to be completed. However, the transportation duration can be padded by simply increasing the total transportation duration. For instance, if the transportation duration is ten hours, and the desire is to add two hours for some other processing, the transportation duration can be extended by two hours to twelve hours. However, there can be master data issues, as the duration must always be added in the future. As a principle of general master data maintenance, whenever possible, the master data should represent what the master data field definition actually says that it is (this field is on Means of Transport Transportation Lane).*

- *Bucket Offset for Production Availability During Shipment: This can be used when the desire is to manipulate the product's availability.*

- *Period Factor for Calculating Availability: Also used to manipulate the availability of the product.*

- *GR Processing Time: This field naturally pads the time when the product becomes available, but should be used for activities within a location (this field is on the Product Specific Transportation Lane).*

- *Addition Stop Duration: This is the correct field to use when the additional time occurs during transportation, but is not part of the actual transportation activity (this field is on the Means of Transport Transportation Lane).*

More on this topic is available at the following link:

http://www.scmfocus.com/sapplanning/2012/11/29/padding-the-transportation-lane/

Non-production Location Processing Times

Non-production Location Processing Times are also maintained on the GR/GI tab of the Product Location Master.

1. *Goods Receipt Processing Time: The time between the delivery or the production of a product and its availability as stock. This time is used, for example, as handling time or time for quality checks, and is added to the transportation duration or the production time of a product. To enable the scheduling of the goods receipt for Production Planning and Detailed Scheduling PP/DS, you must specify a handling resource in the master data for the location.*

   a. *For Planned Orders: In the SNP optimizer and the SNP heuristic, Goods Receipt Processing Time is considered if it is set in the following location: in Customizing for Advanced Planning and Optimization → Supply Chain Planning → Supply Network Planning (SNP) → Basic Settings → Maintain Global SNP Settings; in the SNP:GR for Plnd Ords field, you have selected Processing Time.*

   b. *For Stock Transfers: If the desire is to apply goods receipt and/or goods issue processing time, GR processing time can be applied in either the Product Location Master or in the Product Specific Transportation Lane. If the GR Processing Time check box is not selected, the system considers the goods receipt time entered in the Product Location Master.*

When a handling resource is used, there is a handling-in resource and a handling-out resource. However, there are only two handling resources per location (one in and one out). To schedule the exact goods receipt processing time, the system uses the calendar of the handling-in resource defined in the location. If there is no handling-in resource, the system uses the receipt calendar defined in the location. The handling resource is a strange configuration necessity, as it is almost never used to constrain or level capacity. Because of this, it is essentially a "connect the dots" configuration item as described in the following article:

   http://www.scmfocus.com/sapplanning/2012/12/06/the-goods-receipt-processing-time-and-the-handling-resource/

The Goods Receipt Processing Time field is used frequently, and accounts for all manner of activities that essentially "pad" the time until the system recognizes a stock-on-hand. The Goods Receipt Processing Time can apply to both transportation movements between locations as well as goods receipt within one location, for instance, from manufacturing.

2. *Goods Issue Processing Time: The time between issuing the product from storage and transporting it. This time is used as handling time or time for quality control, and is added to the transport duration (Supply Network Planning and PP/DS) of a product. This is the same field as the Goods Receipt Processing Time but in reverse. Similar rules apply for handling resources as was described for the Goods Issue Processing Time.*

3. *Transportation Lead Time: The transportation lead time is used in SAP APO for vendor managed inventory (VMI) orders to calculate the transportation planning date starting from the loading date. If you have not maintained the transportation lead time in the product master, the transportation lead time is the same as the loading date. This field should probably be called the "VMI transportation lead time." VMI functionality is not enabled that frequently in APO, so this field is not populated very often.*

4. *Pick/Pack Time: The Pick/Pack Time is used in SAP APO for VMI orders to calculate the loading date from the requirement date or material availability date. If you have not maintained a pick and pack time in the product master, the loading date is the same as the requirement date. The same issue applies here as with the previous field in terms of frequency of use.*

Transportation Calendar

The Transportation Calendar declares when transportation activities can be scheduled and works in the same way as the location and resource calendars. The vehicle planning calendar determines the exact working hours and days. Use this calendar to define the time stream in customizing. As described above, the transportation calendar is assigned to the Means of Transport Transportation Lane.

Supply Planning Timings Related to TLB

The transportation load builder (TLB) is the functionality in SNP that follows the deployment planning run. TLB converts confirmed stock transport requisitions into stock transport orders, as well as builds loads from sending locations based upon the transportation equipment (the weight capacity of the truck and the volume capacity of the truck). When in the TLB view, one can bring up these equipment details by selecting the TLB Parameters button.

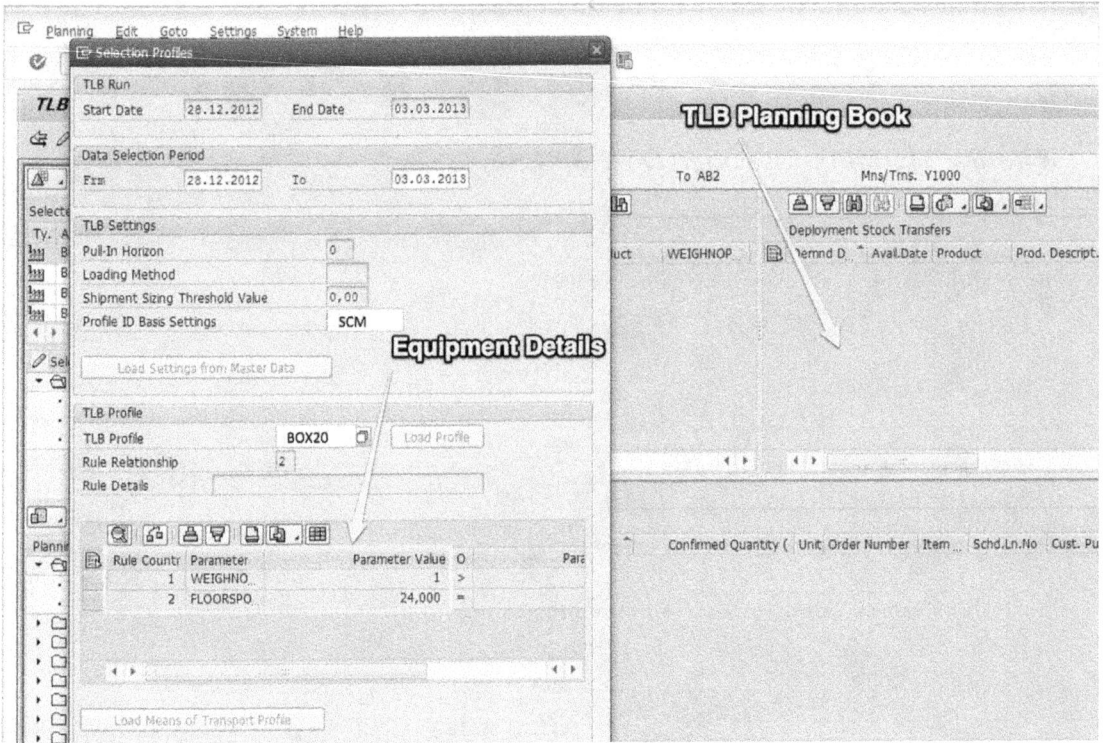

The TLB profile is actually assigned to the means of transport transportation lane.

1. *TLB: Pull-In Horizon: In this field, specify the number of buckets (added to the currently-processed bucket) that the TLB can take into account to look for deployment stock transfers from future buckets. The system looks for deployment stock transfers when it performs shipment upsizing. Used if there are not enough deployment stock transfers in the currently processed bucket to fill up a TLB shipment. The latter case only applies if you selected the Upsizing to Maximum checkbox in Customizing for Advanced Planning and*

Optimization, under Supply Chain Planning → Supply Network Planning (SNP) → Basic Settings → Make TLB Basic Settings. Your master data settings determine whether the TLB performs shipment upsizing. You make these settings on the SAP Easy Access screen, under Advanced Planning and Optimization → Master Data → Transportation Lane → Transportation Lane, in the Means of Transport screen area, in the TrspChangeDecision (TLB: Decision Basis for Shipment Sizing) and Change Thresh.Val. (TLB: Threshold Value for Shipment Sizing) fields. For more information, see the field help for these fields.

Storage Bucket and Planning Bucket Profiles

As I discussed in Chapter 2: "DP Horizons, Calendars and Timings," both DP and SNP share the same requirement for a Storage Bucket and Planning Bucket Profile. DP and SNP can share the same specific Storage Bucket and Planning Bucket Profiles. As this topic was included in the previous chapter and these profiles work the same way for SNP as they do for DP, I will not cover them again in this chapter. Please refer to Chapter 2 for this topic.

When Using CTM

When using CTM, these settings interact with the CTM Time Stream/Planning Calendar. Interestingly, this works in the exact opposite direction as the other time streams/calendars with the periods to the current date at the top. Actually, the setup of the CTM Time Stream/Calendar is in my view more logical than the Planning Bucket Profile.

The CTM Time Stream/Calendar is shown in the screen shot on the following page:

Start

○ Fixed Start Date [ ]

◉ Relative Start [ ] Days

☐ Start from Day of Week [0] 🗓

Define Planning Periods

(1) Period Type [1] Days

No. of Periods [14]

(2) Period Type [2] Weeks

No. of Periods [10]

(3) Period Type [ ]

No. of Periods [ ]

(4) Period Type [ ]

No. of Periods [ ]

The graphic below shows how these timing configurations interact:

Storage and Planning Bucket Profiles, and the CTM Planning Calendar

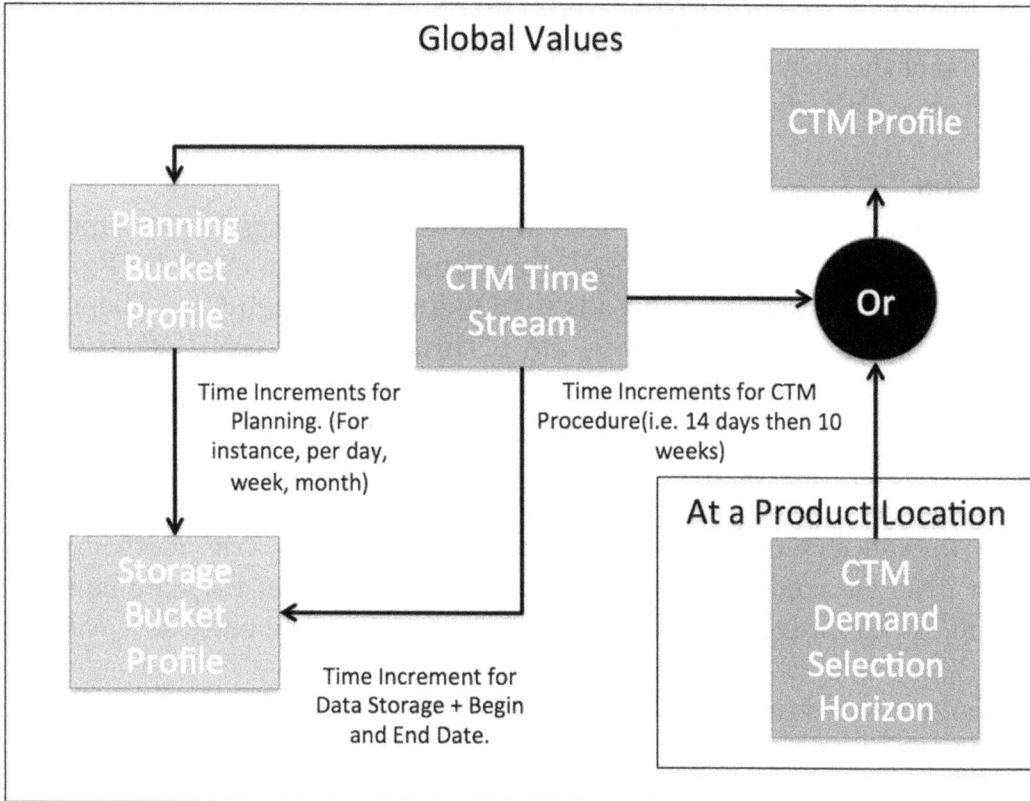

Global Values

Planning Bucket Profile

CTM Time Stream

CTM Profile

Or

Time Increments for Planning. (For instance, per day, week, month)

Time Increments for CTM Procedure(i.e. 14 days then 10 weeks)

At a Product Location

Storage Bucket Profile

Time Increment for Data Storage + Begin and End Date.

CTM Demand Selection Horizon

Production Lead Times

SNP represents the lead times that are carried in the PPM and PDS. SNP can be implemented without PP/DS, which essentially owns these master data elements. On most implementations, SNP and PP/DS work off of the same PPMs or PDSs. However, some projects attempt to use two sets of PPMs or PDSs. Even when they use the same PPMs and PDSs, SNP and PP/DS use them differently. SNP uses them at a higher level, while PP/DS uses them at a more detailed level. There is a way to have SNP treat the PPMs and PDSs as PP/DS does, and this is covered in Chapter 9: "Timing Integration Between DP, SNP, PP/DS and GATP."

The important thing to consider is that SNP represents the production lead times that it shares with PP/DS. As the PPM and PDS are maintained by PP/DS, the discussion of the lead time settings in these objects is located in Chapter 4: "PP/DS Horizons, Calendars and Timings."

Conclusion

There are four planning threads that are performed in supply planning. Three of these threads are covered by SNP functionality. Of the three SNP planning threads, two of the planning threads (S&OP and the Rough Cut Capacity Plan, and the Initial Supply Plan) can use any of three methods (SNP Heuristic, CTM or the SNP Optimizer). One thread—deployment—can use two methods (the SNP Deployment Heuristic or Deployment Optimizer). Each of these threads or planning runs tend to have a different planning horizon, with deployment having the shortest planning horizon and the S&OP planning run having the longest. This chapter showed how the planning horizon is set in each of the method profiles, and how different copies of the profiles can be saved so that they can be rerun at any point in the future, and also scheduled on a recurring basis as a batch job.

This chapter covered time streams/planning calendars for CTM, the SNP Optimizer as well as the timing for how SNP deals with the forecast. This chapter also covered the timings related to deployment, which meant covering the timing setting in the Deployment Heuristic and the Deployment Optimizer. At some point during the project, all of the planning horizons in all of the modules (DP, SNP, PP/DS, GATP) must be understood in relation to one another. The normal progression on projects is for each module area to determine its internal timing, and then during successive solution architecture reviews, the comprehensive picture of timings is brought forward. And in most cases, this takes too long to happen, and can result in mismatches between the timings within the different modules. Pulling the integrated timing discussions forward tends to help projects, and I have used several graphics that have been shown in this chapter to do just that.

All of the methods for all of the planning threads interact with the Product Location Master, and most of the fields for SNP on the Product Location Master are in the SNP 2 tab. SNP has the most master data parameters of any of the modules in APO, which is why profiles were developed exclusively for the SNP 2 tab. They are very helpful, but a bit strange in that they are not externally defined, but defined within the Product Location Master itself. This chapter discussed the fact that some of the field combinations to the profiles don't make much sense.

SNP works just like DP with respect to Storage Bucket Profiles and Planning Bucket Profiles. Both modules require these objects to be filled out, and use them the same way, albeit in different planning books. DP planning books include the forecast toward the bottom of the planning book, as the forecast is the result of activities that are a consequence of demand planning activity, adjustment, etc. On the other hand, SNP planning books generally start off with the final forecast as the first row/key figure at the top of the planning book because the final forecast is the beginning point for supply planning. However, this chapter did not show the setup of the Storage Bucket Profile or Planning Bucket Profile as they were covered in Chapter 2: "DP Horizons, Calendars and Timings."

This chapter also covered the time-related settings and the master data profiles that control many of the time settings in the Product Location Master. The chapter then moved on to the topic of how to create time streams/calendars, and then to the lead-time related supply planning timings. The most prominent of these lead times are those for procurement, production and stock transfer. Procurement lead times can come from the Procurement tab of the Product Location Master or from the Transportation Lane (if the vendor locations are modeled in SNP). The production lead times come from the PPM/PDSs, and the stock transfer times come from the Transportation Lane. Additionally, there are location-specific lead times such as the goods issue and goods receipt. The Goods Receipt Processing Time can be taken from the Product Location Master or taken from the Transportation Lane.

This chapter also covered supply planning timings related to lead times. One of the most important is procurement lead times, which are fairly straightforward to set up. A second type of lead time is encapsulated in the transportation lanes. There are different master data screens in APO for transportation lanes: the

Transportation Lane Header, the Product Specific Transportation Lane, the Means of Transport, the Product Specific Means of Transport, and the TSP (Transportation Service Provider) for Means of Transport. Each one of these master data categories represents a dimension of the transportation lane, and has fields that are specific only to that dimension. These master data categories are both assigned to one another and also have other external master data and configuration objects assigned to them. In all of the master data categories, in addition to the external objects that are assigned to the transportation lane master data categories, there are hundreds of fields that are related to the transportation lane. This is an important fact to understand because this book only showcases the timing related fields. This level of detail provides a great degree of customizability and high level of control over how the transportation lanes behave, but also comes at a cost of considerable complexity. This is complexity that mostly goes unaddressed in the published material in this area. Therefore, this book added several learning aids that should help readers to better understand transportation lanes from their multiple aspects.

The final lead times that were discussed in this chapter were production lead times. Production lead times are used by SNP in order to create both the initial supply plan and the initial production plan. Both SNP and PP/DS work off of the same production lead times.

CHAPTER 4

PP/DS Planning Horizons, Calendars and Timings

The topic of the timings for PP/DS is a bit different than that for DP or SNP. For instance, the PP/DS planning horizon differs from the planning horizon in DP or SNP. While there can be a number of DP or SNP planning runs—each with a different planning horizon—the same planning horizon applies for all locations in the supply network—at least for a particular run (it is possible to use different SNP runs to apply different planning horizons to different product location combinations—but I have never heard of such a thing. Generally one planning horizon is applied for DP and SNP within a single version). However, the same cannot be said for PP/DS, as each factory can have a different planning horizon in PP/DS, and it is not at all uncommon to have different PP/DS horizons per plant, as different plants have different needs and make different things for the company. Therefore, effort may be required to set some of the PP/DS timings so that they are customized per plant. This topic is covered in Chapter 9: "Timing Integration Between the DP, SNP, PP/DS and GATP."

Understanding the Planned (Production) Order Creation Process

One of the complicating factors in implementing both SNP and PP/DS is that both SNP and PP/DS create planned orders. However, which module has created the planned order can always be determined within the planning book by going into the detail view of any planned order. This is because planned orders created by SNP and those created by PP/DS are different order categories. This traceability of order, stock, requirements, etc. is one of the strengths of APO in general. The planned order or planned production order will always be created for PP/DS by SNP regardless of whether planned orders exist in the SNP production horizon. The simple rule about the SNP production horizon versus the PP/DS planning horizon is that orders that are created outside of the SNP production horizon are created as SNP planned (production) orders.

According to SAP Help, the following are necessary for SNP to create the planned order:

- The planned order does not previously exist in SAP APO.

- MRP procedure X (without planning, with BOM explosion) is assigned to the header material of the planned order in SAP R/3.

- The availability date of the header material lies outside the SNP production horizon.

- This is neither a planned order of the type VP (forecast), nor a planned order for project stock or sales order stock.

- The SNP production horizon is maintained on the SNP 2 tab page in the product master (transaction /SAPAPO/MAT1). — **SAP Help**

Most of the PP/DS timing fields are on the PP/DS tab of the Product Location Master. These fields include the following:

Product	White Wine		Base Unit	BTL
Prod. Descript.	White Wine			
Location	San Jose			

| ATP | SNP 1 | ⊙ SNP 2 | ⊙ Demand | ⊙ Lot Size | ⊙ PP/DS | ⊙ Procurement | ◂ ▸ ▢ |

Planning Procedure

| PP Plng Procedure | 2 | Manual Without Check |

Procurement Planning

☐ Part of a Package

Planning Package		□
Product Heuristic		□ ▣
Int. Sourcing Profile		□

Miscellaneous			Order Creation		
Show Production Unit			Plan Explosion		Priority	0
Planning Group			BOM Explosion Date			

Horizons

Opening Period		Conversion Rule	
PP/DS Plng Time Fence			
Adjustment Horizon		Forecast Horizon	0
Rqmts Ascertain. Horizon			
SNP Production Horizon	0		
PP/DS Horizon			

Characteristic Based Deployment

Depl. Char. Profile	
Fair Share Rule	
Pull Deployment Horizon	
Push Deployment Horizon	
SNP Checking Horizon	

1. *Opening Period in Days: The production calendar for the location is a decisive factor in determining the opening date. This field is used to convert orders for SAP ERP.*

2. *PP/DS Production Planning Horizon: How far out into the future the production plan processes for the factories. The production planning horizon is sometimes set per factory. It is set in the production planning system, but interacts with the supply planning horizon, in particular when planned production orders are created by the supply planning system versus the production planning system. In this field, you specify a location-product-specific PP/DS horizon. The production planning horizon can be inherited from the SNP Production Horizon by entering no value in the PP/DS Horizon field. If you do not enter any value for the PP/DS horizon,*

or if you enter the duration "0," the system automatically uses the SNP production horizon as the PP/DS horizon. Therefore, the PP/DS horizon is as long as the SNP production horizon. The graphic that appears below this field section shows the SNP Production Horizon and the PP/DS Production Horizon. The following lists the implications of using the SNP production horizon as the PP/DS horizon:

   a. *The planning intervals for SNP and PP/DS are sequenced with no gaps or overlaps.*
   b. *If the SNP production horizon also has a duration of "0," the system uses the PP/DS horizon from the planning version. You can use the PP/DS firming horizon within the PP/DS horizon to firm (short-term) planning for planning with procurement planning heuristics. SNP is permitted to plan outside of the SNP production horizon only. If the SNP production horizon is smaller than the PP/DS horizon, the planning horizons of SNP and PP/DS overlap. SNP and PP/DS can both use this overlapping period for planning.*

3. *Product-specific Planning Time Fence: Period during which planning can take place with PP/DS. This control is set at the product-location combination and overrides the setting that is applied for the entire model. However, a time fence can also be specified in the Product View.*

4. *Determination of the BOM Explosion Date: Determines when the BOMs are exploded. The indicator specifies which date is to be used for the explosion of the PVSs/BOMs for assemblies and their components. Requirements' planning explodes the BOM or iPPE data for the assembly on a multi-level basis with the BOM explosion date adopted from APO.*

5. *Adjustment Horizon: This horizon is relevant to planning related to sales orders, where you only convert procurement proposals (planned orders and purchase requisitions) into manufacturing orders or purchase orders if these procurement proposals are used to cover sales orders. Using specific Production Planning and Detailed Scheduling heuristics, you delete planned independent requirements for which there are no sales orders, and adjust the purchase requisitions and planned orders used to cover these planned independent requirements accordingly. To adjust the planned independent requirements and procurement proposals for selected products, you use the standard heuristic SAP_PP_015. This heuristic executes the adjustment for all procurement proposals that start in the adjustment period. You can define the adjustment period using the adjustment horizon. Using the standard heuristic SAP_PP_016, you execute the adjustment for selected orders. The adjustment horizon and the adjustment period are not relevant here.*

6. *SNP Production Horizon: SNP Production Horizon in which SNP and CTM do not plan production. This definition is quite long, so I have broken into a "focus on" section below.*

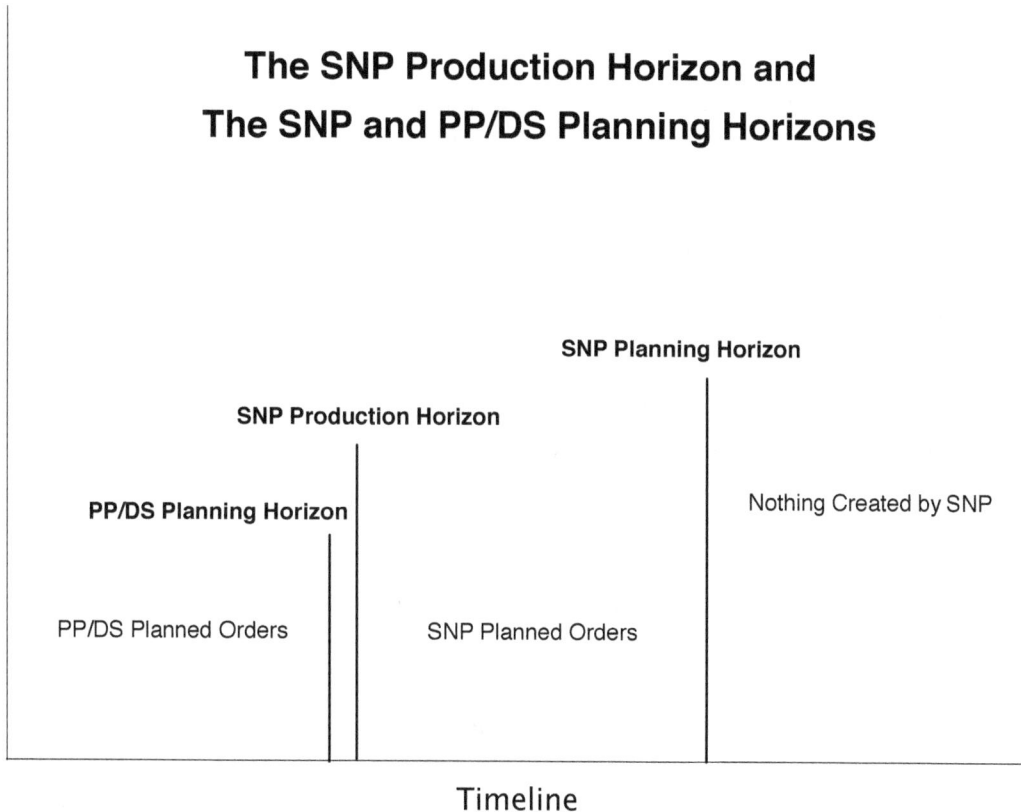

The SNP Production Horizon and
The SNP and PP/DS Planning Horizons

SNP Planning Horizon

SNP Production Horizon

PP/DS Planning Horizon

Nothing Created by SNP

PP/DS Planned Orders

SNP Planned Orders

Timeline

You plan production with SNP or CTM outside of the SNP production horizon; planning is bucket-oriented and usually stretches over the medium-term horizon. In the short-term horizon—that is the PP/DS horizon—you plan production in more detail using automatic Production Planning and Detailed Scheduling (PP/DS). You can manually create PP/DS orders outside of the PP/DS horizon. Therefore, the SNP production horizon is only relevant for SNP and CTM and does not cause constraints on order generation at the PP/DS level.

If the SNP production horizon is shorter than the PP/DS horizon, the planning areas overlap. This means that planning tasks require full reconciliation. SNP does not create any planned orders in the Production (planned) key figure, but moves production to the first day after this horizon. SNP deletes all unfixed SNP planned orders from previous planning runs within this horizon. The horizon starts on the system date (or date defined in the Planning Start Date field of the planning book or using the PDATE user exit for background processing). CTM does not generate or delete any planned orders within this production horizon. The horizon starts on the system date (or the date you specified as the planning start in the CTM profile).

If no value has been specified here, CTM takes into account the PP/DS Horizon in the planning version. If you do not enter any value for the PP/DS horizon or if you enter the duration "0," the system automatically uses the SNP production horizon as the PP/DS horizon. Therefore, the PP/DS horizon is as long as the SNP production horizon, meaning that the planning intervals for SNP and PP/DS are sequenced with no gaps or overlaps. The graphic below this field description section shows the SNP Production Horizon and the PP/DS Production Horizon.

On the PP/DS Tab there are several timing settings that are just copied over from the SNP 2 Tab. I do not list them or describe them here as they have already been described in Chapter 4: "SNP Horizons and Timings." It may seem strange (I know I certainly find it strange), but PP/DS can create STRs with an MRP run (which is a PP/DS heuristic—SAP_MRP_001). To see all the heuristics, view this post:

http://www.scmfocus.com/sapplanning/2008/09/21/ppds-and-snp-heuristics/

And, as of SCM 7.0, PP/DS can now also create confirmed STRs by performing deployment (although it is only meant for characteristic-based planning, or CBP, which is almost never used).

The new PP/DS heuristic can consider the "characteristic values of the receipt and the requirement element for allocating the quantity." This requires that the following take place:

1. The Planning Area 9ASNP-PP/DS be initialized for the current planning version.

2. The heuristic SAP_DEPL_SNG, SAP_DEPL_MUL performs the deployment run for PP/DS and creates the confirmed STRs based upon the fields in the characteristic-based deployment area of the PP/DS Tab.

3. The SAP_DEPL_SNG, SAP_DEPL_MUL heuristic is executed from the Product View, which is where heuristics can be executed interactively for a single product location combination, by selecting the variable heuristic options.

I could keep showing how this works, but I consider this functionality to be a waste of time. First, companies very rarely use CBP in APO. Certainly, if a company wanted to achieve the same results as CBP, there are far better solutions and I am not convinced that CBP is actually sustainable. Secondly, by enabling PP/DS with supply planning functionality, but for a little-used functionality, SAP development has further increased the complexity of PP/DS in a way that will benefit a vanishingly small number of clients. An increasing problem with APO is that the modules are overlapping into each other. When PP/DS can perform supply planning activities, and GATP can trigger production orders, the whole solution becomes more confusing.

The SNP Production Horizon and
The SNP and PP/DS Planning Horizons

SNP Planning Horizon

SNP Production Horizon

PP/DS Planning Horizon

Nothing Created by SNP

PP/DS Planned Orders   SNP Planned Orders

Timeline

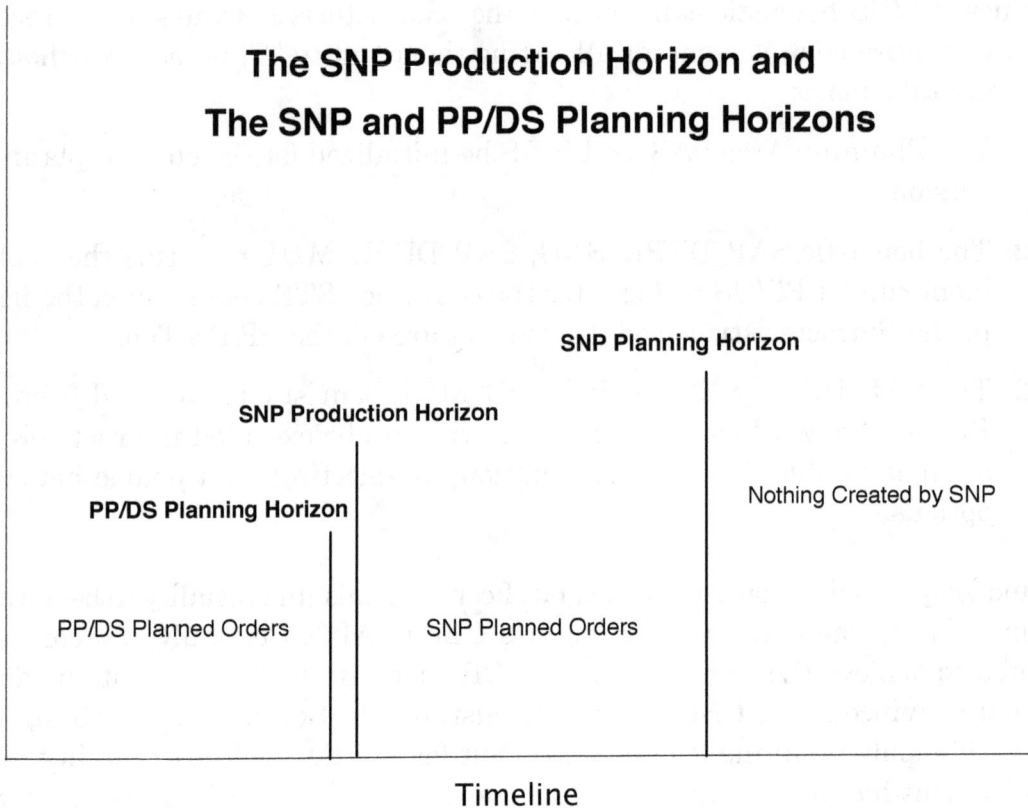

Here is the graphic which shows the relationship between the various planning horizons. We will cover more detail on this topic in Chapter 9: "Timing Integration Between the DP, SNP, PP/DS and GATP."

The Factory and Distribution Center Calendars

The factory and distribution center calendar defines the days available for planning in the factories and the distribution centers. These calendars declare when the locations are available for operation, and serve as a type of constraint. However, in the case of production resources, which are frequently modeled in both SNP and PP/DS, the resource typically sets the lower of the capacity constraints—and therefore is the real constraint. The resources are of course assigned to the location. Supply planning resources are not that frequently activated, but when they are, the similar rule applies.

The Frozen Period

The "frozen period" is a misnomer, as similar types of timing settings in SNP are referred to as "horizons." Therefore, one would normally think to call it the frozen horizon, as it is the horizon over which the planned production orders may not be changed. This appears in the planning book as blue colored cells that are frozen. Why have a frozen period? The reason is explained well by this quotation from PlanetTogether—a best-of-breed production planning and scheduling vendor.

Introducing too much volatility into the schedule in the short term creates "nervousness" on the shop floor, causing inefficiencies and confusion later in the schedule.

Of course, there are also material implications to changing the production schedule at the last minute, in that the semi-finished and component materials may not have sufficient lead time to supply the changed production schedule.

Conclusion

Planned orders are created by both SNP and PP/DS, but which module has created the planned order can always be easily traced within the system. The time settings in PP/DS are considerably less numerous than in SNP and most of them are located on the PP/DS tab of the Product Location Master. PP/DS is commonly implemented with SNP, in fact I would go as far to say that PP/DS implementations without SNP are uncommon, with stand alone SNP implementations without PP/DS being somewhat more common, and these modules work very closely together and share the same resources. Of course they both work off of resource timings, which are described in the next chapter. More on how PP/DS and SNP work together from a time setting perspective is covered in Chapter 9: "Timing Integration Between DP, SNP, PP/DS and GATP."

CHAPTER 5

Resource Calendars and Timings

We will begin this chapter by covering the connection between resource type and planning time orientation. Unfortunately, SAP's explanation of the connection between resource type and the planning time orientation (time-continuous or bucket) is quite confusing. The quotation below is one of the more clear on the topic from SAP.

> *The planning time orientation determines at what level of detail the planning is desired to be in. Longer range planning should be set to bucket-oriented planning, and this means that it uses SNP PPMs (production process model) or PDSs (production data structure which are containers for the resources). Shorter range planning, where the detail of the resources is necessary for a more accurate plan, promotes the use of time-continuous planning, and this means using PP/DS PPMs or PDSs. — SAP Help*

Understanding how the settings must be made in order to make SNP and PP/DS work together is critical, but unfortunately the information that is available on this topic makes understanding this topic much more difficult than it really needs to be. However, this chapter will help, and you can find more details on this topic in the following articles:

http://www.scmfocus.com/sapplanning/2012/08/19/where-ppds-stops-and-snp-starts-with-respect-to-time-and-location/

http://www.scmfocus.com/sapplanning/2012/08/19/time-continuous-planning-versus-bucket-in-ctm-and-ppds/

http://www.scmfocus.com/sapplanning/2009/04/24/pds-vs-ppm-and-implications-for-bom-and-plm-management/

http://www.scmfocus.com/sapplanning/2009/05/03/scm-ppm-and-pds-as-used-in-different-modules/

http://www.scmfocus.com/sapplanning/2012/07/27/the-connection-between-boms-routings-work-centers-in-erp-and-ppms-pdss-in-apo/

Understanding Resources

Resources represent the various capacities within both supply and production planning. SNP can use all the resource types (as SNP can use production resources in addition to supply planning resources), while PP/DS can only use production resources. Therefore, instead of covering resources separately in SNP and PP/DS, it made more sense—to me at least—to dedicate a chapter to resources.

Time Settings on the Resource

The following time-related settings can be found for the various resources that can be set up in APO.

- Single
- Single-Mixed
- Multi-Mixed
- Production Line
- Line Mixed* (Only used in IPPE, not frequently used)

- Bucket

- Vehicle* (Only used for TP/VS, so not covered in this book)

- Transportation* (Used in SNP, but infrequently used as transportation is rarely a hard constraint)

- Calendar* (Not frequently used)

- Calendar Mixed* (Not frequently used)

In this chapter I will cover timing-related fields for the resource types listed above, except those with an asterisk next to them.

While each resource has its own set of tabs and time-related fields, most of these fields are identical or similar. Rather than repetitively listing all the timing-related fields for each resource, I will list the similar timing fields for all of the resources, but note where there are differences. Additionally, I will highlight those resources that have timing fields that other resources do not.

First, let's define some of the resources that appear in this chapter and that are integral to understanding the different resource classifications. We will define the following types of resources:

- Bucket versus Time-Continuous Resources

- Mixed Resources

- Single versus Multi-Resources

- Single-Mixed versus Multi-Mixed Resources

Bucket versus Time-Continuous Resources
A bucket resource has a quantity capacity that is planned on a daily basis and would be defined as something like "400 bottles per day." A bucket-oriented resource is based upon a Bucket-Oriented Dimension, the options of which are:

- Area

- Density

- Electrical Current

- Energy

- Force

- Frequency

- Length

- Mass

- Mass flow

- Power

- Pressure

- Speed

- Temperature

- Time

- Volume

After you have selected a Bucket-Oriented Dimension, you then select the unit of measure for the dimension. This is different to a time-continuous resource, as noted below:

1. *Time-Continuous Planning:* This is applied to PP/DS PPMs and PDSs and provides the highest detail available within APO. However, PP/DS can be set up as a bucket capacity, and in this case, it is necessary to set up a Single-Mixed resource. The PP/DS Bucket Capacity Tab exists on only this time-continuous planning resource type.

2. *Bucket-Oriented Planning:* Bucket-Oriented Planning uses the SNP PPM or PDS, which is more abstract.

Technically speaking, SNP can use time-continuous resources, in that they can be set up in the system. However, as SNP does not schedule below the day, it makes little sense to have SNP use a time-continuous resource.

This topic is explained further at the following link:

http://www.scmfocus.com/sapplanning/2012/08/19/time-continuous-planning-versus-bucket-in-ctm-and-ppds/

Mixed Resources

The nature of the bucket versus time-continuous resource also relates to the topic of the mixed resource. As I have stated, SNP uses bucketed resources, while PP/DS uses time-continuous resources. However, a mixed resource can be set with both bucketed time master data parameters and time-continuous master data parameters. SAP provides the following, highly illuminating quotation on the topic of mixed resources:

> *If you want to consider the resource loads caused by PP/DS orders in SNP planning, and adjust the SNP planning accordingly, you must use mixed resources (single-mixed resources or multi-mixed resources). In mixed resources, you define the bucket capacity for period-oriented planning in SNP and the time-continuous capacity for time-continuous planning in PP/DS. An SNP order utilizes the bucket capacity of a mixed resource and a PP/DS order utilizes the time-continuous capacity of a mixed resource. For SNP planning, the amount of bucket capacity utilized by PP/DS orders is displayed as an aggregated capacity requirement. SNP planning can therefore take account of the PP/DS orders. For PP/DS planning, the time-continuous capacity used by SNP orders is not displayed.* — **SAP Help**

Therefore, a mixed resource has both bucket and time-continuous master data parameters (both for timing—which are discussed here, but also for other settings not covered in this book). A mixed resource can be used for both SNP and PP/DS—that is two different applications, but one resource. However, each application uses the resource—or looks at the resource—in its own way, which helps to explain how production resources that are shared by SNP and PP/DS can be the same. This is a very common question on projects.

Single (Activity) versus Multi (Activity) Resources

After the difference between multi-resources and non-multi resources is made clear, there is a distinction between single or mixed resource. A single resource only allows one activity to be performed at one time on the resource, while a multi-resource allows more than one activity to be performed at one time.

Single-mixed or Multi-mixed Resources

Single-mixed and multi-mixed resources work in the following way:

1. *Single-mixed Resource:* This resource can only process one activity at a time, but can be used by both SNP and PP/DS because this resource type has both time-continuous and time-bucketed master data. (Actually, this resource type can be used for time-bucketed planning for both PP/DS and for SNP, or time-continuous planning for PP/DS and timed-bucketed planning for SNP.)

2. *Multi-mixed Resource:* This resource can process multiple activities at a time, but can be used by both SNP and PP/DS because this resource type has both time-continuous and time-bucketed master data. (However, unlike the single-mixed resource, this resource can only be used for time-continuous planning for PP/DS.)

Resource Settings and What This Means for Time Continuous versus Bucket Planning

Different resource types, such as single-mixed and multi-mixed, can be set up to be used by both SNP and PP/DS. However, how the resources are used can change in SNP depending upon the setting. As is highlighted in the quote below, both time-continuous and bucket-oriented planning can use mixed resources.

> *If you want to consider the resource loads caused by PP/DS orders in SNP planning, and adjust the SNP planning accordingly, you must*

*use mixed resources (single-mixed resources or multi-mixed resources). In mixed resources, you define the bucket capacity for period-oriented planning in SNP and the time-continuous capacity for time-continuous planning in PP/DS. An SNP order utilizes the bucket capacity of a mixed resource and a PP/DS order utilizes the time-continuous capacity of a mixed resource. For SNP planning, the amount of bucket capacity utilized by PP/DS orders is displayed as an aggregated capacity requirement. SNP planning can therefore take account of the PP/DS orders. For PP/DS planning, the time-continuous capacity used by SNP orders is not displayed. — **SNP Help***

The system can automatically derive the bucket capacity of a mixed resource from the time-continuous capacity. Since you do not plan with so much detail in SNP (for example, you do not use sequence-dependent setup times), you can reduce the bucket capacity derived using a loss factor. You obtain such a buffer for detailed planning in PP/DS.

For single-activity resources, multi-activity resources and calendar resources, or for the available time-continuous capacity resources of mixed resources, always enter a rate of resource utilization of 100 percent and a break duration of 00:00:00. Otherwise, liveCache determines a different duration than does CTM planning for the corresponding activities. This may cause the system to fulfill the demand too late.

*CTM always prefers to plan activities overlapping on multi-activity resources and does not support the synchronization of activities. Ensure that the No Synchronization setting in the resource master on the Planning Parameters tab page under SyncStart. Otherwise, the SAP liveCache executes a synchronization for the corresponding activities. — **SAP Help***

This is shown in the graphic below, which emphasizes and reinforces these points:

Resource Types and Their Function

Function		Single	Single-Mixed	Multi	Multi-Mixed
	Can Represent Both Time Bucketed and Time Continuous Resources	No	Yes	No	Yes
	Can Perform More than one Operation at a Time	No	No	Yes	Yes
	Can Represent Both Time-Bucketed and Time-Continuous Resources, as well as Specifically Time-Bucketed Resource for both SNP and PP/DS	No	Yes	No	No

Now that we have covered the basic commonly used resource types in APO, we can get into the next layer of detail, which is the timing fields that are on each resource.

Timing Fields Per APO Resource Type

Fields	On Which Tab?	Single	Single-Mixed	Multi	Multi-Mixed	Production Line	Bucket
Time Zone	General Data	Yes	Yes	Yes	Yes	Yes	Yes
Factory Calendar	General Data	Yes	Yes	Yes	Yes	Yes	Yes
Days +	General Data	Yes	Yes	Yes	Yes	Yes	Yes
Days 1	General Data	Yes	Yes	Yes	Yes	Yes	Yes
Start	Time Contin. Capacity	Yes	Yes	Yes	Yes	Yes	No
End	Time Contin. Capacity	Yes	Yes	Yes	Yes	Yes	No
Break Duration	Time Contin. Capacity	Yes	Yes	Yes	Yes	Yes	No
Synchronization Start	Time Contin. Capacity	No	No	Yes	Yes	No	No
Time Buffer	Time Contin. Capacity	Yes	Yes	Yes	Yes	No	No
Productive Time in Hours	Time Contin. Capacity	Yes	Yes	Yes	Yes	Yes	No
{Base Rate} Per	Time Contin. Capacity	No	No	No	No	Yes	No
Period Type	SNP Bucket Capacity	No	No	No	No	No	Yes
Number of Periods	SNP Bucket Capacity	No	No	No	No	No	Yes
{Valid From} Start	Downtimes	Yes	Yes	Yes	Yes	Yes	Yes
{Valid To} End	Downtimes	Yes	Yes	Yes	Yes	Yes	Yes

As can be seen from the previous matrix, most of the resource types have the same timing fields. The exception here is the bucket resource, which has two timing fields. No other resource type has and does not have any of the Time-Continuous Capacity fields.

Interestingly, the resources are given the option of either using a set-up matrix or a synchronized start.

The Time Orientation Flexibility of Capable to Match (CTM)

A good example of what we just covered is found in CTM. Within APO there are three methods for supply planning: the SNP Optimizer, the SNP Heuristic, and Capable to Match (CTM). However, of the three, CTM can also be configured to perform not only supply planning, but also production planning—creating planned orders that are native to PP/DS (rather than requiring conversion from SNP to PP/DS). CTM has this ability primarily because it has been designed by SAP to work in either the bucketed or the time-continuous orientation.

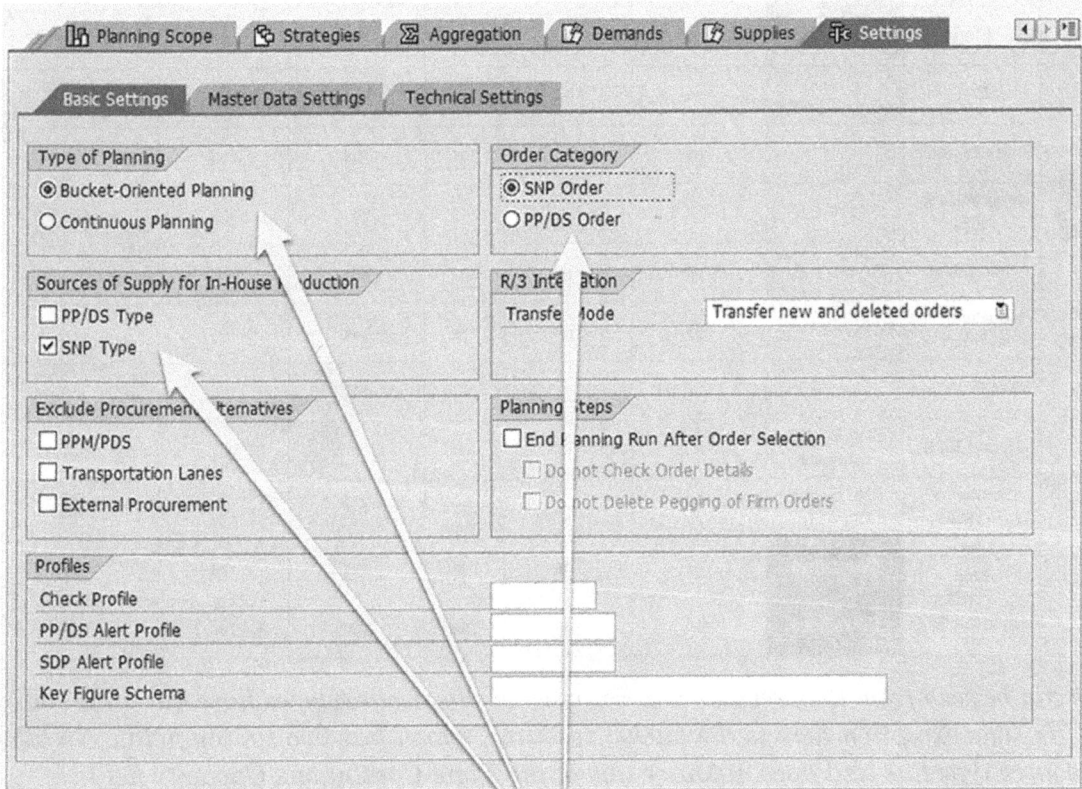

Three settings for bucket-oriented planning.

Here you can see that the CTM Profile can be set to run in either SNP "mode" or PP/DS "mode." In order to switch between modes, the settings above would be changed. In the screen shot I have SNP type planning enabled, but by switching to the other option for each setting, I could convert to PP/DS mode. I would also require time-continuous resources that CTM could work with.

This functionality has been active in CTM for some time; however, I have never seen it enabled at a client. It brings up some interesting questions.

1. *Acceptance of the CTM Prioritization?: CTM in PP/DS mode would directly prioritize the planned orders based upon the CTM prioritization logic, as explained in these articles: http://www.scmfocus.com/sapplanning/2012/06/05/ctm-customer-priorities-versus-order-priorities/ http://www.scmfocus.com/sapplanning/2009/12/08/customer-prioritization-and-ctm/*

2. *Would PP/DS Procedure Be Used After the CTM PP/DS Run?: CTM can be capacity-constrained, so a CTM run in PP/DS mode would result in a feasible plan, and one for which no conversion of SNP orders to PP/DS orders would be required. However, at this point, would the company want to run any heuristics in PP/DS on these planned orders? It would seem that if a company were dedicated to the CTM prioritization sequence, that the next step would be to manually manipulate the CTM-generated planned orders in the PP/DS detailed scheduling board.*

3. *What Would be the Duration of the CTM Production Planning Horizon?: In most cases, a production planning horizon is somewhere between two and four weeks. However, in this case, the production planning horizon could be as long as the supply planning horizon. In addition, there would be no purpose in setting a value for the production planning horizon, as there would be no overlap between the supply planning horizon and the production planning horizon (as is normally the case when SNP and PP/DS are co-implemented). Instead, there would be a single combined supply and production planning run. I could see (as is stated in the bullet point above) that PP/DS is only used to make manual changes through the PP/DS detailed scheduling board. That would be one design. Another design could have PP/DS heuristics used, and in that case, the supply versus production planning horizon and the overlap would again be an issue.*

4. *CTM may be able to work in a bucket-time orientation and can create PP/DS orders; however, it cannot do things like incorporate a set-up matrix, something that PP/DS can do (see this article on the changeover planning http://www.scmfocus.com/productionplanningandscheduling/2010/12/06/changeover-planning-in-sap-ppds-vs-planettogether/). Therefore, CTM cannot be as accurate as PP/DS. On the other hand, most companies that I have worked with have problems effectively implementing the set-up matrix in APO, and may fall back to emulating the set-up*

times with a production cycle, so this would seem to be a more hypothetical than real problem. For companies that want a solution that is effective at managing setup/changeover times, there are much better solutions than PP/DS.

The Conversion of SNP Planned Orders to PP/DS Planned Orders

The PP/DS orders that are created by CTM can be used without conversion when time-continuous planning is used in CTM, as described in the quotation below:

> *Mixed resources have both the SNP bucket and PP/DS time-continuous capacity definition. CTM planning can use mixed resources for planning. When planning in PP/DS mode, CTM uses the time-continuous capacity as the primary capacity for finite planning. The bucket capacity is calculated for the scheduled activity to keep the time-continuous and bucket continuous capacity requirement consistent. On the other hand, when planning in SNP mode using mixed resources, the bucket capacity is used for finite planning, but time-continuous capacity isn't calculated. — **Capable to Match (CTM) with SAP APO**

Therefore, if a CTM Profile is required to process in time-continuous mode for a month or two, and then process in bucket-oriented planning mode, it often makes sense to break the planning horizon up with two CTM Profiles that are identical except for the time orientation and which PPMs and PDSs are used (SNP for bucket-oriented and PP/DS for time-continuous).

The Resource Timing Field Definitions

1. *Time Zone: The time zone describes the location of an object in relation to its local time. The time difference of the time zone in hours/minutes relative to the UTC.*

2. *Factory Calendar: The factory calendar defines workdays and non-workdays.*

3. *Days +: Defines the end of the validity period of the available capacity of the resource.*

4. *Days (–): Defines the start of the validity period of the available capacity of the resource. Starting from the day on which the resource is created (or the planning relevant resource data is changed and saved), the system counts the given number of days into the past. You should define the time period relevant for scheduling a resource to be as short as the planning considerations allow. By doing so, you avoid using too much memory in SAP liveCache.*

These are the time-related fields for the Single-Mixed resource. New fields appear on this tab depending upon the type of resource.

1. *Start: Start time of the working day.*

2. *End: End time of the working day.*

3. *Break Duration: The duration of breaks where resource is not working.*

4. *Productive Time in H: A calculated field based upon the three previous fields. The total time the resource is available for work.*

1. *Synchronized Start: This defines whether the system synchronizes the start times of activities on multi-mix resources and multi-activity resources when these activities have the same duration and a further identical characteristic. When synchronizing, the system schedules the new activity either at the same start time as an activity with the same duration and characteristic (which has already been scheduled) or, without overlap, before or afterward. By synchronizing, you can create blocks of activities on the multi-resources that can be processed simultaneously because they have the same duration and characteristic. You specify the value of the characteristic by using a set-up group or a set-up key that you assign to the operation in the production process model. These are the alternatives: no synchronization, synchronization.*

a. *If you select "No synchronization," the system schedules activities on multi-resources with overlaps. The system only executes synchronization for multi-resources that you only use as primary resources in the modes of production process models. Synchronization can be used to model the loading of an oven. Because the oven can only be loaded or unloaded all at once, you must ensure that it is filled to full capacity with products that require the same temperature and duration. Therefore, you can only schedule activities for the oven that have the same durations and require the same temperature. Activities with a different duration or temperature can only be loaded into the oven without overlap either before or afterward. You can model different temperatures using different set-up keys that you assign to the operations, and hence to the activities of the operation. — SAP Help*

2. *Time Buffer: You use the time buffer in Production Planning and Detailed Scheduling as a safety time to protect the resource or the activities processed on the resource from unforeseen delays in material staging.*

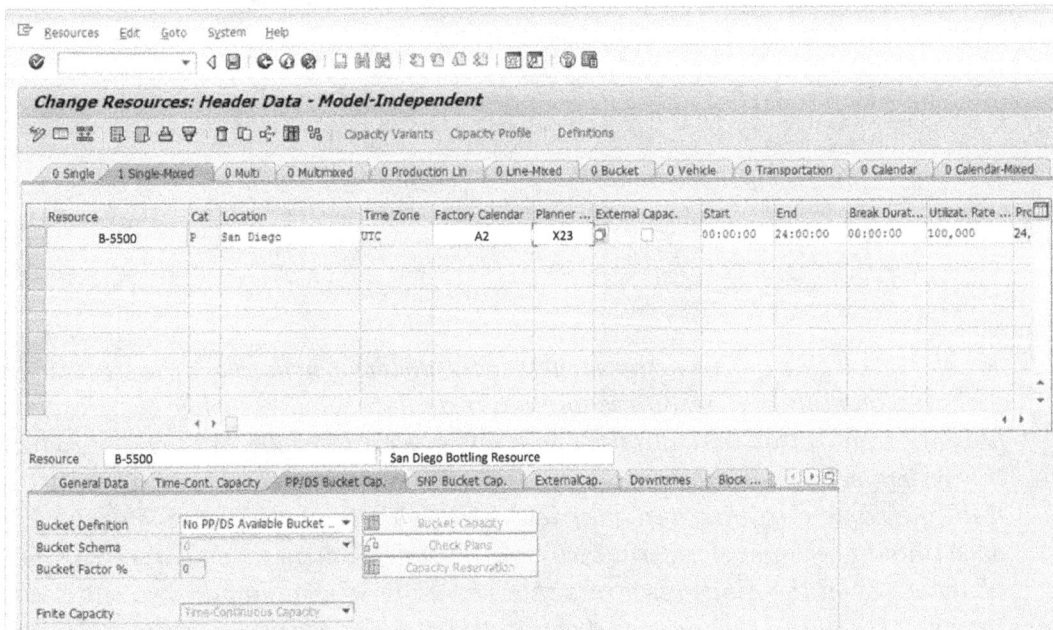

Both the Resource PP/DS Bucket tab and the Resource SNP Bucket tab have the same time-related fields. So I have simply put them below the next screen shot.

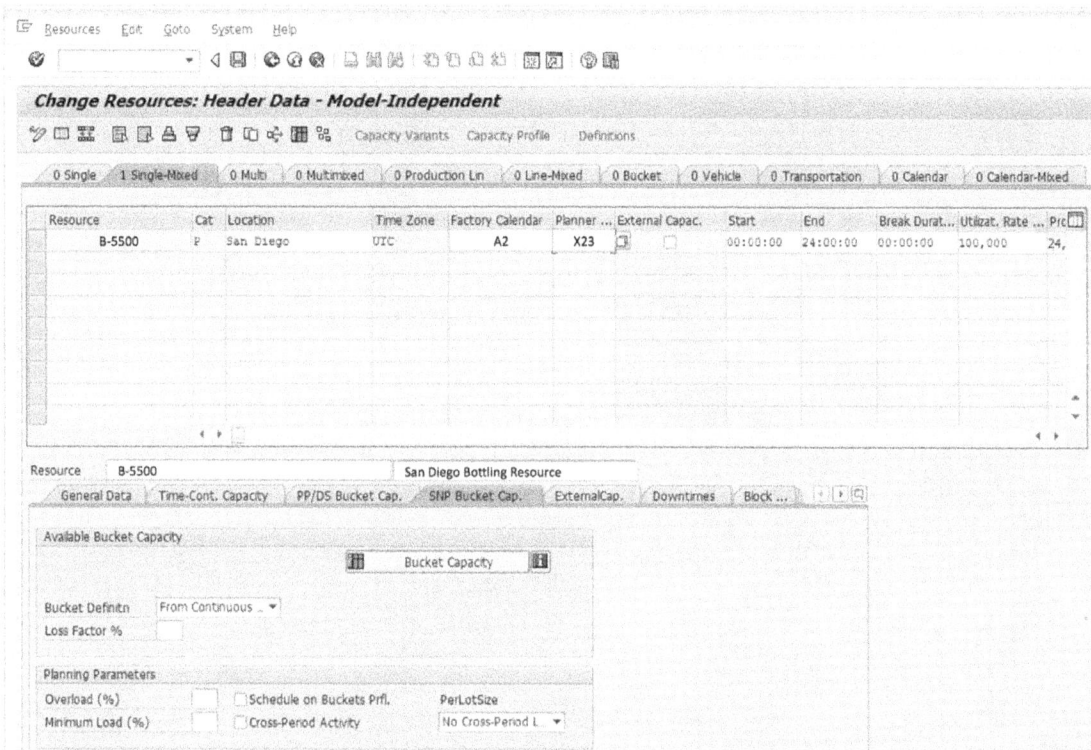

1. *Bucket-Oriented Dim: Sets the dimension of the resource. Options include: (w/o dimension), Area, Density, Elec. current, Energy, Force, Frequency, Length, Mass, Mass flow, Power, Pressure, Speed, Temperature, Time, Volume. I include this field because time is one of the options.*

2. *Bucket Definition: The bucket can be either from continuous capacity, which in that case all that is necessary is to add a loss factor (in the field shown in the screen shot). In order to achieve the same allocation in a single or multi-activity resource and bucket resource capacities can be adjusted using this loss factor.*

3. *Schedule on Buckets Profile: Activities can only begin at the start of the bucket.*

4. *Cross Period Activity: Specifies that an activity may start in one period and in another. If his indicator is not activated and activities exist in SNP that last longer than the bucket (day), the system cannot schedule these activities.*

When the Definition is set to "Maintain," the following timing fields appear on the SNP Bucket Capacity tab.

1. *Period Type: Determines whether the capacity applies to a time period (bucket), thereby describing, for example, a production rate or usage rate.*

2. *Number of Periods: Number of days to which you apply the capacity. By applying the capacity to a time period, you describe, for example, the production rate or usage rate of the resource.*

Downtimes

Another way to adjust the capacity downward is by adding downtimes. Downtimes are typically added for scheduled maintenance. The downtimes are adjusted in the Downtimes tab.

Downtimes can be added in the Downtimes tab as shown above.

1. *Valid From: Day downtime begins.*

2. *Start Time: Time downtime begins.*

3. *Valid To End: Day downtime ends.*

4. *End Time: Time downtime ends.*

PPM and PDSs and Resources

Production Process Models (PPMs) and Production Data Structures (PDSs) are containers for resources, bill of materials and routings, as described in the graphic below:

BOMs, Routings, Work Centers and the PPM and PDS

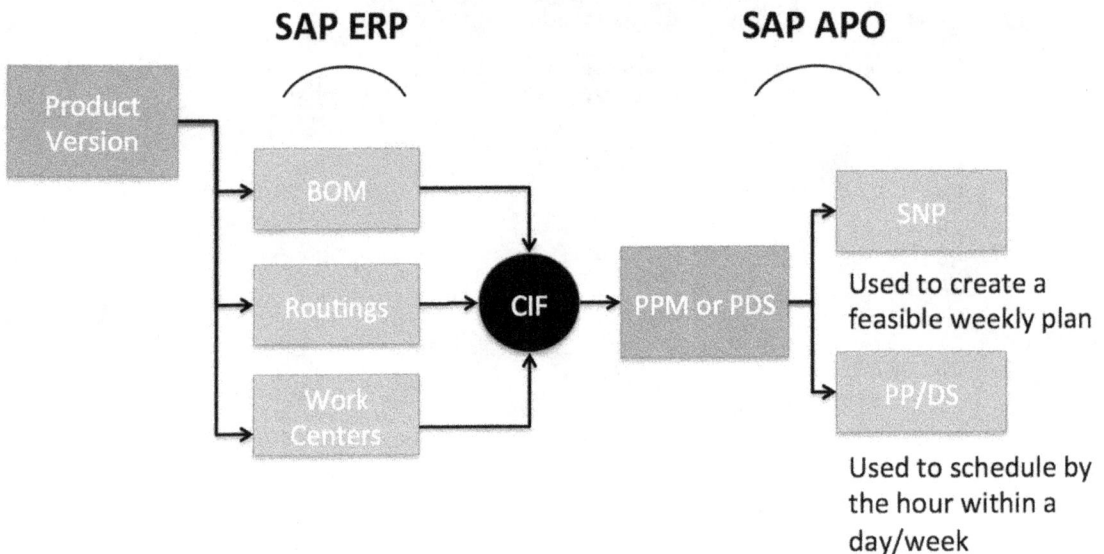

While sometimes SNP and PP/DS use different resources, in most cases they use the same resources, although they are in fact duplicated in the system—that is there is both an SNP and a PP/DS production data structure (PPM or PDS) created from a Production Version in SAP ERP.

Here in the PDS transaction in APO, we can see that a PDS comes in different "flavors." (I only have one selected in the screen shot above because my screen capture program causes the drop down to disappear—however, the options I list below can all be selected in this transaction.) The two most common options are the SNP and PP/DS PDS; however, the following PDS usage types exist:

1. *PDS for Supply Network Planning (SNP)*

2. *PDS for Production and Detailed Planning (PP/DS)*

3. *PDS for Demand Planning (DP)*

4. *PDS for CTM Planning (CTM)*

5. *Template PDS for Industry-specific Optimizer*

All of these PDS "flavors" began as the same Production Version over in SAP ERP.

While SNP represents the PPMs and PDSs in its model, in most cases the PPMs and PDSs are determined and loaded by the PP/DS team. The primary time element within the PPM and PDS is the resource. The following graphic shows a resource screen shot. Resources can be stated in terms of time or buckets. Most of the time, PP/DS tends to work off of resources that are set to time-continuous.

Bucket resources, which state the capacity in terms of a quantity, are common in process industries. One example of a bucket resource is a tank resource, which could be set at a capacity of 10,000 gallons. When time-continuous resources such as in the screen shot example below are entered into PP/DS, they can be used by SNP; however, SNP essentially treats them as if they are bucketed. This is in fact the most common way to use time-continuous PP/DS resources in SNP. This topic is covered in detail in Chapter 5: "Resource Calendars and Timings."

Notice from this screen shot that timing which is productive is set for that resource per day. The best way to think of this is as an average, because these values can be adjusted per day.

If you select the "Capacity" button you will be taken to where the individual day rates can be altered.

Mon	Week	Day	Date	Start	End	Break	Prod.Tm.	Capacity	Util. Rate	Start of Shift	Not a Workda
		WE	20.06.2012	08:00:00	16:00:00	00:30:00	7,50	2.000,000	100,000	✓	☐
		TH	21.06.2012	08:00:00	16:00:00	00:30:00	7,50	2.000,000	100,000	✓	☐
		FR	22.06.2012	08:00:00	16:00:00	00:30:00	7,50	2.000,000	100,000	✓	☐
	26	MO	25.06.2012	08:00:00	16:00:00	00:30:00	7,50	2.000,000	100,000	✓	☐
		TU	26.06.2012	08:00:00	16:00:00	00:30:00	7,50	2.000,000	100,000	✓	☐
		WE	27.06.2012	08:00:00	16:00:00	00:30:00	7,50	2.000,000	100,000	✓	☐
		TH	28.06.2012	08:00:00	16:00:00	00:30:00	7,50	2.000,000	100,000	✓	☐
		FR	29.06.2012	08:00:00	16:00:00	00:30:00	7,50	2.000,000	100,000	✓	☐
July	27	MO	02.07.2012	08:00:00	16:00:00	00:30:00	7,50	2.000,000	100,000	✓	☐
		TU	03.07.2012	08:00:00	16:00:00	00:30:00	7,50	2.000,000	100,000	✓	☐
		TH	05.07.2012	08:00:00	16:00:00	00:30:00	7,50	2.000,000	100,000	✓	☐
		FR	06.07.2012	08:00:00	16:00:00	00:30:00	7,50	2.000,000	100,000	✓	☐
	28	MO	09.07.2012	08:00:00	16:00:00	00:30:00	7,50	2.000,000	100,000	✓	☐
		TU	10.07.2012	08:00:00	16:00:00	00:30:00	7,50	2.000,000	100,000	✓	☐
		WE	11.07.2012	08:00:00	16:00:00	00:30:00	7,50	2.000,000	100,000	✓	☐
		TH	12.07.2012	08:00:00	16:00:00	00:30:00	7,50	2.000,000	100,000	✓	☐
		FR	13.07.2012	08:00:00	16:00:00	00:30:00	7,50	2.000,000	100,000	✓	☐

1. *Capacity Leveling Horizon: When a single step supply planning procedure such as allocation or optimization is used, there is no capacity leveling and therefore no capacity leveling horizon. However, if MRP or a supply planning heuristic is used, the capacity leveling horizon is set in a capacity leveling profile which allows the horizon to be controlled per capacity leveling run. In most cases, this horizon will match the horizon of the initial or network supply plan; however, it does not necessarily have to. Where the initial supply planning horizon is longer than the capacity leveling horizon, a portion of the supply network will not be capacity-leveled. This is shown in the following screen shot.*

2. *Extended SNP Production Horizon: To be discussed in Chapter 9: "Timing Integration Between DP, SNP, PP/DS and GATP."*

3. *SNP Production Horizon: Also to be discussed in Chapter 9: "Timing Integration Between DP, SNP, PP/DS and GATP."*

Resource Calendars

This is when the resources—either production or supply planning resources—are actually available to perform work.

There are four basic resource categories: P (Production), T (Transportation), S (Warehouse), and H (Handling Resource). The resource types are shown along the tabs: Single, Single-Mixed, Multi, Multi-Mixed, Production Line, Line Mixed, Bucket, Vehicle, Transportation, Calendar, and Calendar Mixed.

The resource view is a nested interface. Tabs show the different resource categories, and specific resources are listed within the individual tabs. One can read the resource line item by line item, or one can look at the tabs that contain the same information as is contained in the line items, but in a different view. Once the specific resource is selected, the second row of tabs applies to that particular resource.

After the calendar is assigned, we can go and check the Time-Continuous Capacity tab.

Some of the information in this tab comes from the factory/resource calendar and some come from the capacity profile. I will discuss the capacity profile a little later in this chapter.

What is shown in this view is the "standard," which is controlled by all the parameters that you see in this screen shot. The capacity variant applies for the days that the resource is active, which is determined by the factory/resource calendar.

By simply making a change in this view, the capacity can be changed for the entire planning period. For example, the utilization can be reduced from 100 percent to

75 percent. Or, if the desire is to change specific days, that can be accomplished by selecting the Capacity Button, which will open the screen below:

Pl. Version					
Resource	Bottling Resource				
Capacity Variant	0	Profile Corresponds to Standard Capacity			
Date	20.06.2012				

	2012/4	2012/5	2012/6
WN	12 13 14	15 16 17 18 19 20 21 22 23	24 25 26 27
MO	19 26 2	9 16 23 30 7 14 21 28	4 11 18 25 2
TU	20 27 3	10 17 24 1 8 15 22 29	5 12 19 26 3
WE	21 28 4	11 18 25 2 9 16 23 30	6 13 20 27 4
TH	22 29 5	12 19 26 3 10 17 24 31	7 14 21 28 5
FR	23 30 6	13 20 27 4 11 18 25 1	8 15 22 29 6
SA	24 31 7	14 21 28 5 12 19 26 2	9 16 23 30 7

Mon	Week	Day	Date	Start	End	Break	Prod.Tm		Capacity	Util. Rate	Start of Shift	Not a Workda
		WE	20.06.2012	08:00:00	16:00:00	00:30:00	7,50		2.000,000	100,000	✓	☐
		TH	21.06.2012	08:00:00	16:00:00	00:30:00	7,50		2.000,000	100,000	✓	☐
		FR	22.06.2012	08:00:00	16:00:00	00:30:00	7,50		2.000,000	100,000	✓	☐
	26	MO	25.06.2012	08:00:00	16:00:00	00:30:00	7,50		2.000,000	100,000	✓	☐
		TU	26.06.2012	08:00:00	16:00:00	00:30:00	7,50		2.000,000	100,000	✓	☐
		WE	27.06.2012	08:00:00	16:00:00	00:30:00	7,50		2.000,000	100,000	✓	☐
		TH	28.06.2012	08:00:00	16:00:00	00:30:00	7,50		2.000,000	100,000	✓	☐
		FR	29.06.2012	08:00:00	16:00:00	00:30:00	7,50		2.000,000	100,000	✓	☐
July	27	MO	02.07.2012	08:00:00	16:00:00	00:30:00	7,50		2.000,000	100,000	✓	☐
		TU	03.07.2012	08:00:00	16:00:00	00:30:00	7,50		2.000,000	100,000	✓	☐
		TH	05.07.2012	08:00:00	16:00:00	00:30:00	7,50		2.000,000	100,000	✓	☐
		FR	06.07.2012	08:00:00	16:00:00	00:30:00	7,50		2.000,000	100,000	✓	☐
	28	MO	09.07.2012	08:00:00	16:00:00	00:30:00	7,50		2.000,000	100,000	✓	☐
		TU	10.07.2012	08:00:00	16:00:00	00:30:00	7,50		2.000,000	100,000	✓	☐
		WE	11.07.2012	08:00:00	16:00:00	00:30:00	7,50		2.000,000	100,000	✓	☐
		TH	12.07.2012	08:00:00	16:00:00	00:30:00	7,50		2.000,000	100,000	✓	☐
		FR	13.07.2012	08:00:00	16:00:00	00:30:00	7,50		2.000,000	100,000	✓	☐

What comes up is a capacity profile, where one can make the adjustments per day or can create another capacity profile.

The Factory and Distribution Center Calendars (Resource Calendars)

The factory and distribution center calendars are the basis for other calendars. The fact that the factory and distribution calendars are assigned to the resource and to planning calendars is indicative of a parent-child relationship. The following graphic shows how this works:

Calendar Interaction

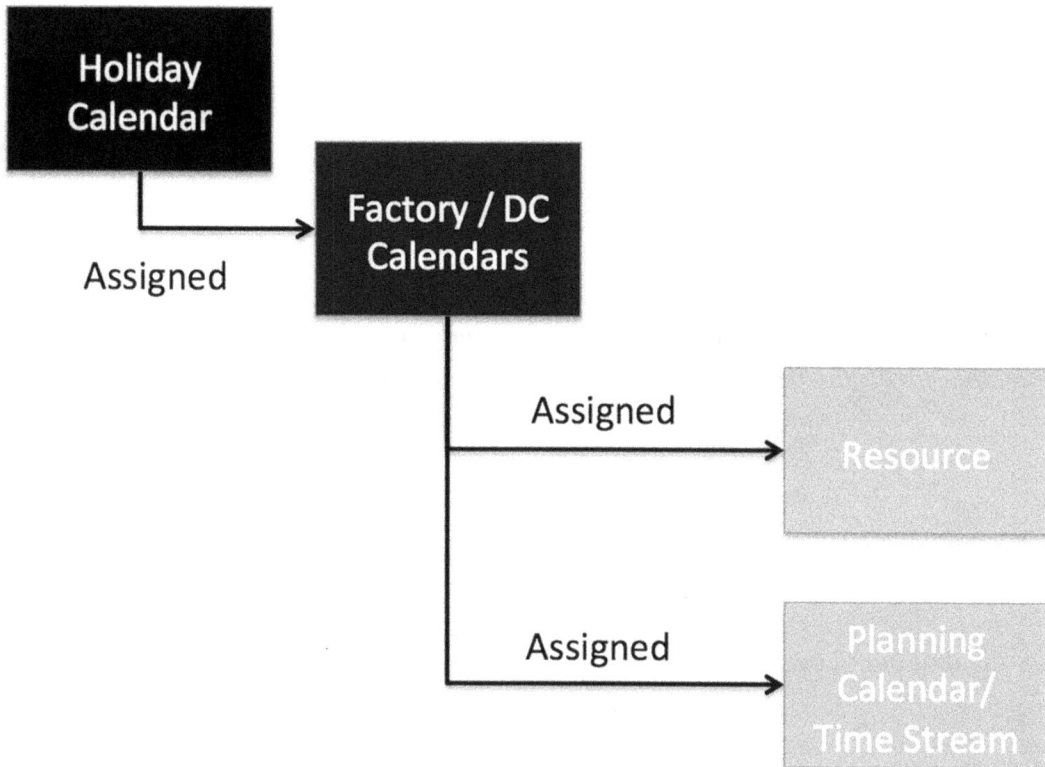

First the factory and distribution calendars are set up, and then they are assigned to resources and to planning calendars. The holiday calendar is in turn assigned to the factory and distribution center calendar. Both the holiday calendar and the factory calendar are created in the same screen.

To begin, we need to create a factory or distribution center calendar.

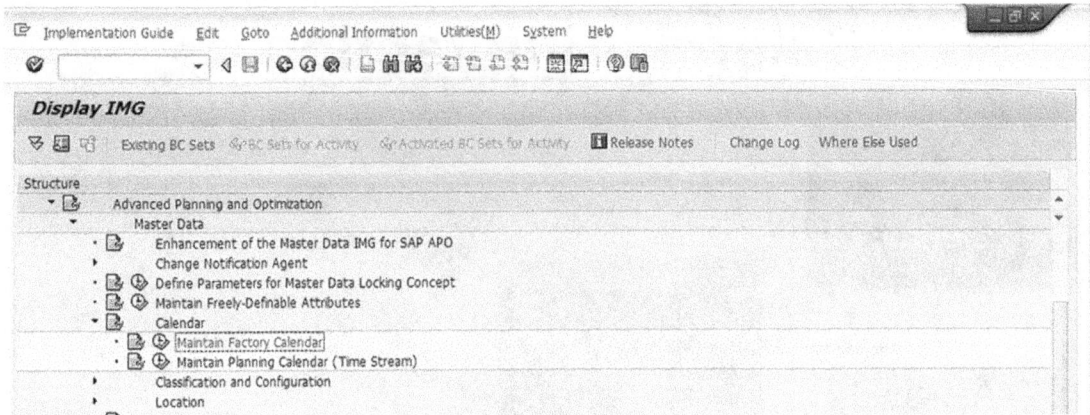

Unlike the planning time streams/location calendars which are set up in SAP Easy Access, the "factory" calendars are set up in the configuration area.

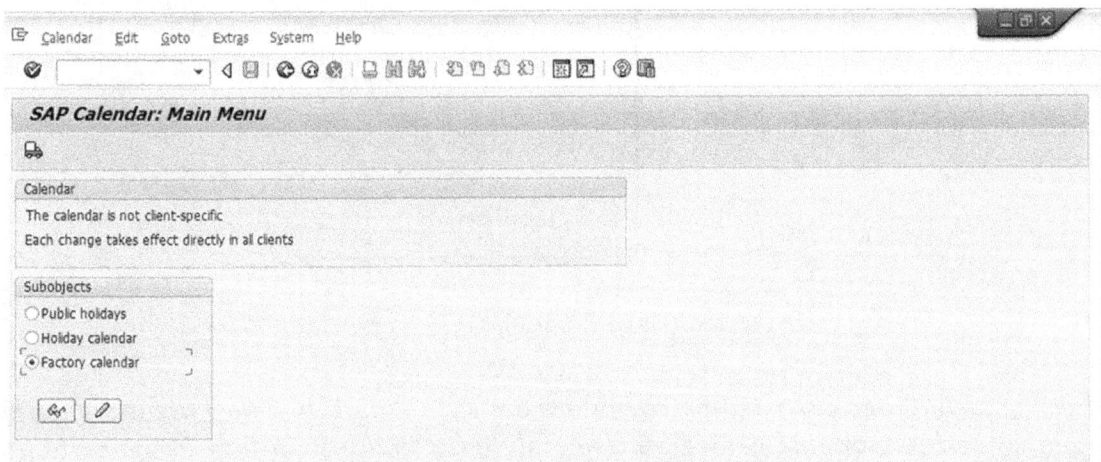

Once inside, we can choose from three different types of calendars: Public Holidays, Holiday Calendars, and Factory Calendar. As I will show in the following screen shot, a factory calendar can have a holiday calendar associated with it. Notice I have saved the factory/resource calendar and called it "Z1."

Once this factory calendar is created, it can be assigned to the resource. I will do this by assigning the "Z1" factory/resource calendar to the General Data Tab of the resource.

Capacity Profiles

SAP has two mechanisms to provide saved alternatives when it comes to capacity. One is the Capacity Profile and the other is the Capacity Variant. SAP has the following to say about the Capacity Profile versus the Capacity Variant:

This (capacity) profile enables you to maintain supply details for shifts and intervals, and has the following advantages over capacity variants:

- *Among other things, you can make changes to times and the rate of resource utilization without having to maintain a new shift or interval. You can see the day to which these changes refer.*

- *The changes refer only to the selected resource, and not to any number of resources. — **SAP Help***

The Capacity Profile does not have its own transaction. Instead, the Capacity Profile is created within the resource transaction. One can go into the Capacity Profile by selecting the Capacity Profile button at the top of the resource screen.

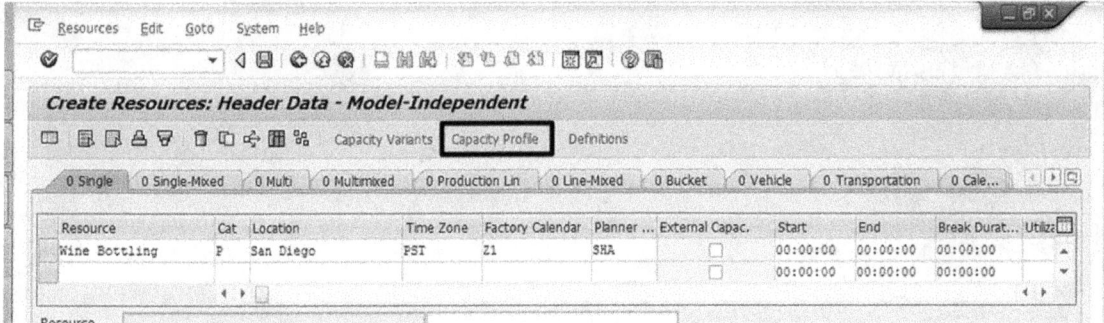

See the Capacity Profile button in the resource view. Fields are the Month, Week, Day, Start, End, Break, Productive Time (Start : End–Break), Utilization Rate, Start of Shift, Not a Workday.

Capacity Variants

The intervals—that is the time for which the capacity variant is valid—must not overlap. Each resource may have up to ninety-nine variants. Variants are designed to model resource capacities that change over time. Variant names are created in configuration, but the information that is entered into the variants is filled out inside of the resource view. You can choose among the variant names, and then assign them to the values such as the workdays, shift sequence, shift factor definition, and the location.

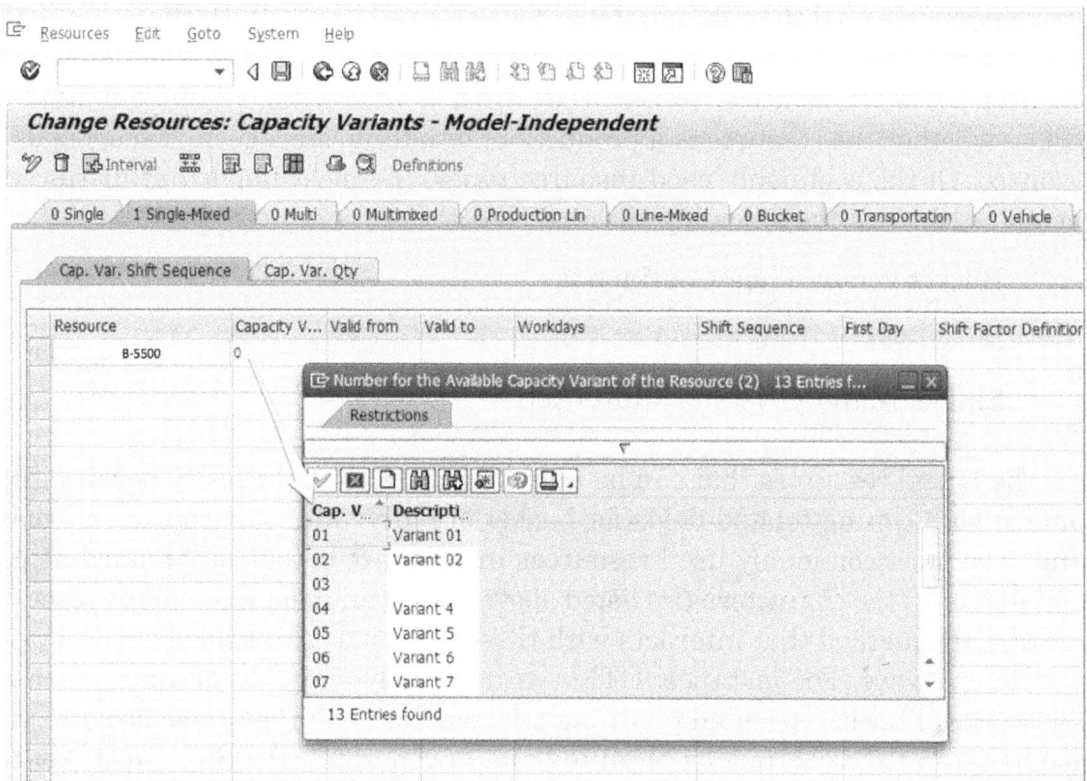

Above, you can see that I have created two capacity variants, each with a different validity period and with a different utilization rate.

Conclusion

Resources represent the various capacities within both supply and production planning. SNP can use all the resource types (SNP can use production resources in addition to supply planning resources), while PP/DS can only use production resources.

This chapter covered the timing-related fields for resources. With the exception of the bucket resource, most of the timing-related fields across the commonly used resource types are identical. Where they differ is in how the resource is used by APO—whether the resource is a production, handling, storage or transportation resource. Of the commonly-used resource types, the most important distinction between them are the following characteristics:

- Bucket versus Time-Continuous

- Mixed versus Non-Mixed

- Single (Activity) versus Multi (Activity)

It is the mixed resources that can be used both by SNP and PP/DS, because they contain both timing-related fields for bucket-oriented and time-continuous planning. The most commonly used resources in APO are essentially named as one combination of the characteristics listed above. However, in addition to the resource timings, the method that interacts with these resources can be designed to work in different ways. For instance, CTM—traditionally a supply planning method that works in bucket-oriented planning and generates SNP planned orders—can also be set to time-continuous planning and to generate PP/DS planned orders.

As with a location, a calendar can have a resource associated with it that determines the workdays of the resource. The resource-available times, which are declared within each resource, then operate within the open days of the calendar. A resource is populated with a capacity, which can be constrained or unconstrained, but the location calendar, resource calendar and the start, end and break duration form another constraint that is as important as the capacity value assigned to the resource.

The resource calendars control when the resource is available for work. First the factory and distribution calendars are set up, and then they are assigned to resources and to planning calendars. (The holiday calendar is in turn assigned to the factory and distribution center calendar. Both the holiday calendar and the factory calendar are created using the same screen.

CHAPTER 6

GATP Planning Horizons, Calendars and Timings

GATP stands for Global Available to Promise. One might ask what the difference is between GATP and the normal ATP that exists in the SAP SD (Sales and Distribution) module. The concept behind GATP was that ATP could be improved by doing the following:

1. Offering better performance and faster response times using much more complex checking logic than is available in ATP.

2. Having more complex rules (rules-based availability checking, which is a series of substitution rules, including for example, location, product, location-product, PPM, etc.).

3. Looking out among multiple locations (ATP in SD can look at one location only).

The theory behind adding the word "global" to "ATP" is that ATP could "search the globe" and return a confirmation from anywhere. This is a marketing hyperbole and an overstatement of how GATP is actually implemented—which is very similar to SAP CTM in that its potential greatly exceeds its implementation in practice. In fact, I have been on several projects where, after months of going around and around on GATP and its requirements, all the company does is re-create SD ATP in GATP. The clients promise themselves that they will double back and implement the design and functionality that was the original reason for the selection of GATP, but they often never do.

None of the books or articles on GATP even hints at the project reality of the product. SAP is coy regarding which parts of GATP are live at existing client sites. Consulting companies certainly don't tell their clients, so it is very difficult for a client to find out how GATP is used, which clients are using it, and which parts of its moderate to advanced functionality are live.

Unable to get companies to successfully implement even much of the moderate functionality in GATP, SAP Development is so sales oriented and unconcerned with implementation success that it continues to enlarge the scope of GATP to the point where it can now do things such as trigger production orders. Every new addition of functionality means more rounds of analysis, more complexity and more cost in the evaluation stage. My observation about the SAP development team for GATP is they are basically very focused on building sand castles to the sky. If they had been serious about making a more implementable product, they could have, but decided to continually pile on more and more esoteric functionality.

Getting back to the "global" aspect of GATP. Most products are not simply sent to "any global location." Instead, most products flow through specific and typically regional and sub-regional supply networks. These networks are economical and are defined in the supply planning system for deployment (the second supply planning run which is performed after the initial supply planning run). Secondly, GATP has many configuration options. However, many of the rules are difficult for the business to define, or at least define in a consistent manner. As a result, GATP is often implemented with a very simple design compared to what it is capable of.

Definitions for the GATP Product Location Master Timing Fields

Most of the timing settings for GATP timing are located on the Product Location Master. An ATP tab also exists for the location master; however, there are no timing-related fields on this view.

The ATP tab describes the connection between the location and SAP ERP (its connection to a Sales Org, etc.) and its prioritization. Timing settings exist at the product-location combination, a screen shot of which is shown on the following page:

1. *ATP: Horizon for Re-creating Receipts in Calendar Days: Defines a time period behind which receipt elements are created via Capable to Promise (CTP) or via a conversion of the ATP tree structure (after a multilevel ATP check) in the order network of the SAP liveCache. The time period consists of check date (today's date) and calendar days that you specify in the horizon for re-creating receipts. By the time you reach this point, you have already performed CTP processing or a conversion of the ATP tree structure (after a multilevel ATP check) and changed the sales order in SAP R/3 (SD), for example. If the requirements date (material availability date) is later than the end of the horizon, then the system attempts to ignore the receipt elements created in a previous check (as long as their status allows this) and to create them within a new ATP check.*

2. *ATP: Checking Horizon Calendar: The calendar for the checking horizon corresponds to a planning calendar (time stream) that you have created in Customizing for master data.*

3. ATP: Checking Horizon in Days: This is probably the most important timing in GATP, and because of this I have a special section on this field, which follows.

Multiple Values GATP Uses for Obtaining the ATP Checking Horizon

GATP can do a number of things—so many in fact that on many projects, GATP after months of exposure and explanation, most clients are trying to figure out how to use it. However, if we boil GATP down to its most basic element we can observe that GATP's primary purpose is to provide confirmations back on sales orders. Therefore, it has a timing setting, which controls how far out it can or will provide a confirmation. This is the order promise horizon and is the ATP Checking Horizon, which is shown in the screen shot below:

The ATP Checking Horizon can be set per product-location combination. However, that is only one way to set this value. While this value may make it appear as if there is only one area where the ATP Checking Horizon is set, in fact, it is not set in simply one location, as is evident from the APO Product Availability Overview transaction. It can also be derived or calculated the following ways:

1. *In-House Production = Replenishment Lead Time*

2. *External Procurement = Purchase Processing Time + Planned Delivery Time + Goods Receipt Processing Time*

In this way, the ATP Checking Horizon can simply be based upon the total lead time, but as you will see later on in this chapter, I question if this is the most logical way to set the ATP Checking Horizon. I am actually in favor of setting the ATP Checking Horizon in the Product Location Master.

ATP: Checking Horizon in Days: Defines a time interval (checking date + period) in which a product availability check can be carried out. If the requirement date lies within this time interval, the check is carried out. Requirements that lie beyond the checking horizon are not checked. You can display the replenishment lead time, for example, using the checking horizon. If you want to include the checking horizon in the product availability check, you need to set the corresponding indicator in Customizing for the product availability check. If you do not use the calendar for the checking horizon, the checking horizon is calculated in days. Otherwise, it is calculated in workdays according to the calendar. If you use SAP APO in connection with an SAP ERP system, the Checking Horizon field is populated with the value for the total replenishment lead time (that you entered in the material master in SAP R/3) when the material master data is transferred. If you have not entered a value for the total replenishment lead time in the SAP ERP system, for products produced in-house the total of the in-house production time and goods receipt processing time that you entered in the material master is adopted in the checking horizon at the time of the data transfer. If you have not entered a total replenishment lead time in the SAP ERP system, for a product procured externally the planned delivery time is adopted in the checking horizon at the time of the transfer. This is the most important timing field in GATP as it is essentially the GATP planning horizon.

Setting the Length ATP Checking Horizon for Make-to-Stock Environments

First, before we get into the details of this section, I want to establish the environment that I will be discussing, which is make-to-stock. GATP can—hypothetically—be made to work in a make-to-order environment, but this then begins to become not available-to-promise but capable-to-promise. I will not cover this environment for several reasons:

1. While many companies want to migrate to a make-to-order environment, in reality, very few companies can do this. Some of the few that do, such as airplane manufacturers and defense contractors, build very expensive and complex products (that is, no procurement until a sales order is booked). These companies literally do not build to a forecast, but must have sales orders. However, these industries have customers that are accustomed to providing sales orders far out into the future. Most of the other companies that do not make these types of products are living in a fantasy land if they think that their customers will accept make-to-order lead times.

2. When GATP is run in a make-to-order environment, this is called capable to promise (CTP) instead of available-to-promise (ATP) and connects GATP to PP/DS—which means checking capacity rather than checking planned stock on hand. CTP has been a popular topic with presales departments in multiple vendors for as long as I have been working in the advanced planning space; however, I have never seen a company actually pull off a CTP implementation. So until proven otherwise (and I have been keeping up to date with several best-of-breed vendors on this topic), I consider CTP to be fool's gold.

Of course, there is the intermediate stage—the stage between make-to-order and make-to-stock—called assemble-to-order, which is attainable for many companies that do not work in the types of industries that I just mentioned. This intermediate stage is where forecasts are created for semi-finished and components that are inputs to finished goods that are not forecasted and only assembled when a sales order is received (think the original Dell model). However, when it comes to the topic of available-to-promise and GATP, given the high risk level of the implementation, it makes little sense to talk about more complex GATP designs, because in practice, these designs just can't seem to be taken live.

Two basic factors should be used to determine the length of the ATP Checking Horizon in a make-to-stock environment. One is how far out in advance customers need to receive confirmations. The second factor—and actually just as important—is the quality of the supply plan. GATP, as with any other availability checking system, is dependent upon the quality and accuracy of the supply chain plan. The probability of an accurate available-to-promise response must be measured against the probability of an inaccurate available-to-promise response. This is described in more detail in the following article:

http://www.scmfocus.com/sapplanning/2012/07/23/gatp-and-the-supply-plan-quality-and-the-order-promise-horizon/

I propose that the length of the ATP checking horizon should mostly be determined by the quality of the supply plan, along with the company's customers' predisposition for ATP accuracy.

However, while many executives want the capabilities provided in GATP, not every company has the plan quality to have a lengthy ATP Checking Horizon. These types of analysis of a company's capabilities should occur, but often do not occur during the sales process. The sales literature describes what GATP is capable of, but the question is not merely about GATP's functionality. GATP cannot improve the supply plan and GATP can never compensate for a poor supply plan (or, of course, a poor demand plan). SAP and consulting companies want to paper over this fact and present the most simplistic picture they can, so that their unsuspecting customers will buy and choose to implement as much GATP as possible. Both SAP and the major consulting companies have significant monopoly power, which means they can behave as they wish, and do not pay long-term consequences for the dissemination of misinformation or of their underperformance because they are not subject to the market forces of a competitive market. The ability to abuse one's monopoly power is the main motivator for gaining monopoly power in the first place—and is why companies never tire of mergers and "synergy."

SAP placed GATP in APO, even though order promising is not a planning function. However, generally speaking, APO has superior and higher performance hardware to SAP ERP, and the type of complex ATP that GATP is capable of does require powerful hardware. GATP requires planning accuracy in order to add value, at least if it is to be used as designed. This brings us to the topic of two alternatives for using GATP:

1. Use GATP to only promise on orders.

2. Use GATP to promise on both orders and on planned orders (including, of course, stock transport requisitions).

GATP for Actual Stock and Orders or Planned Stock and Planned Orders?
GATP is designed to perform confirmations back on sales orders into the future, and that is for planned future stock. This planned stock is generated by SNP, and is in some cases based upon forecasts and in other cases is based upon reorder points. One might ask the question:

How can future or planned stock be based upon reorder points if reorder points only kick off orders when actual stock drops below the reorder point level?

This is actually an excellent question, and the answer is that the reorder points in SNP do not work off of actual stock only, but also off of planned stock or "projected stock on hand." How this works is described in the following article:

http://www.scmfocus.com/sapplanning/2012/07/27/reorder-points-in-sap-apo-and-its-stock-calculation-method/

Plan Quality and How to Configure GATP to Work
GATP is designed to work off of "projected stock-on-hand," which is the output of the supply plan. This is one reason that the reorder point calculation basis is different in SAP SNP than it is in SAP ERP. The two different calculation

approaches for the reorder point are not related to what the reorder point uses for its determination or the alternatives presented in the Product Location Master. Instead, the options are related to whether the reorder point forward calculates or does not forward calculate beyond the replenishment lead time—that is, how far forward in time does the reorder point look? However, as no supply plan is 100 percent accurate, a rational question would be:

Does this not mean that some customers will receive a confirmation, and then end up not receiving their promised stock?

The answer is "yes." Does it also mean that some customers that actually could have been satisfied will be turned away, possibly months before their orders are required, so that they go to competitors? Yes, running GATP off of projected stock-on-hand means this as well. However, the concept of GATP is that value is added by being able to look out and provide confirmations on sales orders based upon the supply plan, only to tell customers that they cannot confirm or deny the sales order because they cannot see that far out. The value added by GATP when used this way, is of course dependent upon how often its confirmations are correct, which is of course only partially dependent upon GATP itself and is more dependent upon the accuracy of the supply plan (which also contains the demand plan and production plan). Regardless of how GATP is set up, over time customers will or will not begin to take confirmations generated by GATP seriously, depending upon how often the confirmations are correct. However, a company's clients should not have to make this determination. Rather, the company implementing GATP should determine how far out GATP should perform order promising, and this should be based upon the estimated quality of the supply plan. They should also publish this information to their customers so that their customers know the general probability of the confirmation they are receiving. Companies that have a low-accuracy supply plan should be discouraged from implementing GATP because its order promising horizon is too far out compared to its actual visibility. These two options—running GATP on the basis of orders or on the basis of orders plus requisitions—are illustrated on the following page:

GATP Based Upon What?

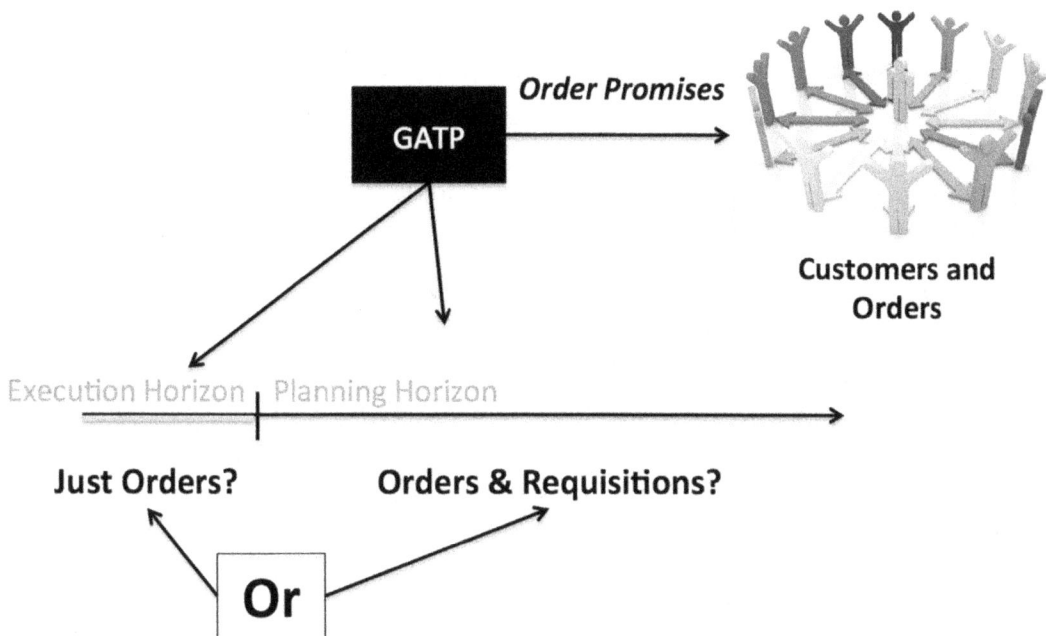

Basing GATP Strictly on Orders
There is a way to run GATP for clients whose supply planning accuracy is lower than acceptable: shorten the ATP Checking Horizon to the point where GATP will only confirm on stock based upon orders (as opposed to requisitions). This method greatly reduces the power of GATP, but it can be the correct choice for companies needing more time to improve their supply planning accuracy.

One common problem for a company implementing GATP along with DP, SNP and PP/DS: what is the estimating the accuracy of the supply plan? Accuracy of the supply plan is very difficult to estimate and depends upon many factors, such as the demand plan, but not the least of which is how effective the company is at running simpler and easier to maintain systems such as SAP ERP. Improved supply plan accuracy upon which GATP is dependent is an expected benefit of any implementation. However, how much will supply planning accuracy improve after the new systems are live? As this is a very difficult question to answer, it is conservative to start out with GATP based upon orders. Once the supply planning accuracy is known, the ATP Checking Horizon can be determined, and once set the ATP Checking Horizon can be changed very quickly. Finally, the ATP Checking Horizon can be set by product-location combination, so the ATP Checking Horizons can be longer for those products that have more accurate supply plans and vice versa.

In addition to the major timings listed previously, GATP also has the following timing:

1. *Selection Horizon in Days: (Conversion of Planned Purchase Orders into Purchase Orders): Specifies the time period (current date plus the specified number of days) in which the start date/time of planned purchase orders should lie, so that the system selects this for conversion. The system selects for conversion those planned purchase orders whose start date/time lies before or within this time interval. The system does not convert planned purchase orders whose start date/time lies after this time interval.*

APO Availability Check Simulation

The availability check simulation is designed to provide the same available-to-promise as if a sales order were sent to GATP and GATP responded to the sales order. This transaction is valuable as it allows a configuration resource to test that GATP is working as expected. It can be used for troubleshooting by those resources that work in order management, deal with customers, and rely upon the results of the GATP. Before bringing an issue to Support, they can access the transaction and see if GATP behaves as reported when a customer comes back with a complaint. The transaction can also be used by order management personnel to submit requests on different dates and in different quantities for their customer to see what the response from the system will be.

APO Availability Check: Simulation: Initial Screen

Product Availability

Product/location

Product	
Location	
Sublocation	
Version	
Special Stock	

Check Control

Requirements Profile		RP Active
Check Mode		Correlation Profile
Business Event		Earliest Correlation Date
With Requirement Quan		PASS Parameters
Rounding Active		Substitution Presel. Active
External Exclusions		

Date/Quantity

- Material Availability Date
- Material Availability Date (Time Stamp)
- Requested Delivery Date
- Goods Issue Date

Date
Time Stamp

Requirement Quantity   Unit

2. *Date: This is the date that you enter into the APO availability check screen. You can specify to the system which of the following dates is being used:*
   a. *Material Availability Date: This is when the product is demanded. It is the most important date in the GATP simulation.*
   b. *Requested Delivery Date: This is when the product must be delivered.*
   c. *Goods Issue Date: This is when the product must be goods issued.*

APO Product Availability Overview

The APO Product Availability Overview transaction shows you, by time bucket, the product availability based upon a selected business event. (A business event is an activity that initiates an ATP check—for example an SD order, SD order (make to stock order), SD Delivery, Checking Rule for Stock Transfer, Planned Order, Process Orders, etc.) Different ATP quantities can be defined for different business events, so for instance ATP quantities may be configured to be available for an SD Delivery, but not a stock transfer, or any number of different scenarios of this type.

There are several important dates on this transaction.

1. *End of Check Horizon: The end of the checking horizon is the date upon which the product could be available again, if production or procurement is started today. The end of the checking horizon is set to the current day if you include the checking horizon in the product master record. The calendar*

for the checking horizon is determined for a specific location in the product master record. The end of the checking horizon corresponds, from a business standpoint, to the end of the replenishment lead time in the R/3 system.

2. *Date: The date for which the various ATP values apply. (Applied to the ATP line item.)*

3. *Time: The time for which the various ATP values apply. (Applied to the ATP line item.)*

To find the other two timing fields, select the Buckets button at the top of the screen.

On this pop-up screen we have the following time-related fields:

1. *Time Zone: This is the time zone for the ATP.*

2. *Start Issue Bucket: The time shift on the ATP bucket issue.*

3. Start of Receipts Bucket: The time shift on the ATP bucket receipt.

4. Start Forecast Bucket: The time shift on the ATP bucket for the forecast.

Conclusion

GATP is an enhanced version of the ATP that exists in the SAP SD module. GATP has a very complex set of functionality. GATP is much higher performance than ATP in the SAP SD module, which was one reason for placing GATP within APO which typically sits on hardware that has higher performance memory than does SAP ERP. However, GATP is rarely implemented beyond a basic level. GATP's primary purpose is to provide confirmations back on sales orders. Many of the GATP timing fields relate to how far a system will look out—either for an actual response, or in a simulation or in reviewing the allocations. The most important time setting in GATP is the ATP Checking Horizon, which can be set at a product-location combination, allowing the horizon to be altered depending upon any factor. Two basic factors should be used to determine the length of the ATP Checking Horizon in a make-to-stock environment. One is how far out in advance customers need to receive confirmations. The second factor—and actually just as important—is the quality of the supply plan. GATP, as with any other availability checking system, is dependent upon the quality and accuracy of the supply chain plan. The most important factor (in my opinion) in making a determination on the proper length for the ATP Checking Horizon is the quality of the supply plan. This is actually rarely brought up as a topic on projects because there is a strong tendency to think in silos regarding the various APO modules—until, that is, toward the end of the implementation. GATP cannot improve the supply plan and GATP can never compensate for a poor supply plan (or, of course, a poor demand plan). GATP is only a "spokesman" for the planning that has occurred already—the lower the quality of the confirmation on the sales order, the lower the quality of the confirmation of the sales order and the less likely the customers are to believe the confirmation. The basic common sense of don't make promises (or too many promises) that you can't keep applies quite nicely to this situation.

There are a variety of ways to determine the ATP Checking Horizon per product-location combination, but one way is to use only orders when going live with GATP rather than planned orders.

CHAPTER 7

Transfer Timings Between SAP APO and SAP ERP

There are a number of important timing settings that control the flow of information between SAP APO and SAP ERP. For instance, transfers of planned production orders can be set to allow only transfers to SAP ERP for planned production orders within the SNP production horizon. This setting restricts the adoption of changes to SNP planned orders from SAP ERP. The default setting is no filtering of planned production orders in SAP APO; APO posts all planned production orders and changes that are sent from SAP ERP. To implement the setting described above, this default must be changed in the Global Settings to "Only allow transfer for planned orders in SNP production horizon."

Transfer Settings from APO to OLTP

The control screen shown on the following page controls transfer from APO to SAP ERP. This screen is called "Transfer to OLTP." OLTP is an acronym for "online transaction processing," which means SAP ERP. To navigate to this screen, click on the following sequence of menus:

SAP Advanced Planning and Optimization (SAP APO) → Supply Chain Planning → Supply Network Planning (SNP) → Basic Settings → Configure Transfer to OLTP Systems.

This screen shot shows how the transfer of orders and requisitions between APO and ERP can be controlled. It can also be controlled by area of the supply planning system (initial supply plan, deployment plan, transportation load building, etc.). Here are some interesting features of this transfer dashboard:

1. *The first group of settings refers to the results of the initial supply plan, and how quickly they should be transferred to SAP ERP. As with several of the settings, it also allows specific order categories to be excluded from the transfer.*

2. *The second group of settings refers to the second online supply planning run, which is deployment. The screen says "Purchase Requisition" and "Purchase Order." However, deployment does not create either of these order categories. Instead, deployment creates stock transport requisitions, but as these are technically purchase requisitions (placed upon an internal location rather than a vendor), you can see that the transfer screen shows them as purchase requisitions and purchase orders.*

3. *The third group of settings controls Transportation Load Builder (TLB). TLB will communicate stock transport orders to ERP.*

4. *The last group deals with the transfer settings for CTM.*

Many other vendors often have transfer dashboards of this type; however, for vendors that do not provide these dashboards, the objects to be transferred can still be controlled by the integration team within the integration harness.

Sending Transaction Data to APO

The Core Interface, CIF, is often associated with transferring master data. However, it also determines the transfer of transaction data.

Create Integration Model

Material Dependent Objects		General Selection Options for Materials		
☐ Materials	☐ Plants	Material	to	⇨
☐ MRP Area Matl	☐ MRP areas ⇨	Plnt	to	⇨
☐ AMPL		Matl Type	to	⇨
☐ Customer Mat. ⇨		PlantSpec. Mtl Stat	to	⇨
☐ Planning Matl ⇨	☐ Supply Area	MRP Ctrlr	to	⇨
☐ ATP Check		MRP Type	to	⇨
☐ SimpleDis ⇨		ABC Indicator	to	⇨
☐ Extern. Plant ⇨				

		Selection of Source of Supply		
☐ Contracts ⇨	☐ SchedAgreements ⇨	☐ Material-Dependent Source of Supply Selection		
☑ Pur.Info Record ⇨		☐ Include Dependent Vendors and Issuing Plants		
		Vendor	to	⇨
☐ PPM ⇨		Create Loc./BP		
☐ PDS (ERP) ⇨	☐ BOM ⇨	Material	to	⇨
		Supplying Plant	to	⇨
☐ Storage Loc.Stk ⇨	☐ Transit Stock ⇨	Selection of Purchasing Info Record		
☐ Sales Ord Stock ⇨	☐ Project Stocks ⇨	Vendor	to	⇨
☐ Cust. Spec. Stk ⇨	☐ Vend. Spec. Stk ⇨	Material	to	⇨
		Purch. Org	to	⇨
☐ Sales Orders ⇨	☐ Sched. VMI ⇨	Plnt	to	⇨
☐ Plan Ind. Reqs ⇨	☐ Req. Reduction	Info Rec. No.	to	⇨
☐ Planned Orders ⇨	☐ Prod. Order ⇨	☐ Standard Info Record		
☐ Prod. Campaign		☐ Subcontracting Info Record		
☐ POs and PReqs ⇨	☐ Manual Reserv. ⇨	☐ Consignment Info Record		
☐ Insp. Lots				

Order Types from SAP ERP

Conversion of Recommendations to Orders within APO

SAP allows the direct creation of purchase orders, production orders and stock transport orders in SAP APO, meaning that purchase requisitions, planned orders and stock transport requisitions can be converted into purchase orders, production orders and stock transport orders within APO, rather than in SAP ERP. In fact, when TLB is used in SNP, this is the standard workflow.

Anyone with a lengthy background in supply chain planning systems knows that this is not how most planning systems are designed. The standard division of responsibilities between planning systems and ERP systems has been that the planning system only recommends and the ERP system decides what to convert. However, while SAP offers many alternatives, SAP seems to be pushing clients toward performing requisition conversion of recommendations inside of APO. There is functionality that is driving this strategy. For instance, if one compares the Stock Requirements List in ERP to the Product View in APO, it is quite clear that the Product View in APO has much richer features. The APO Product View shows pegging and has many more specific and information-rich tabs than ERP's Stock Requirements List, making a strong argument that APO has better views than ERP, and therefore is the superior environment in which to perform requisition conversion. What is so surprising about this is that SAP, which was so against planning systems before it had APO, has become so interested in promoting more and more use of APO over their ERP system. Back in the 1990s, when SAP ERP was co-implemented with a planning system (and I worked for an advanced planning vendor), SAP implementation managers were very resistant to changing anything in ERP's design to account for the recommendations provided by the planning system. At that time, SAP implementation managers seemed to view the planning system as some small insect flying around their ERP system, and if the client forced them to, they would agree to integrate it. However, times have certainly changed, and SAP now views its ERP system as more of a commodity. SAP can only charge upgrade prices for SAP ERP to existing clients, but if their ERP clients purchase APO (or another noncore product) they receive higher revenues. Thus, for some time SAP has had a powerful financial incentive to push clients to buy APO. This shows how financial incentives drive software development. And, if I add my experience with multiple vendors into the mix, I think that most opinions held by those who work at software vendors are not really philosophical at all, but are simply based upon the approach that the particular vendor has to sell.

Very simply, SAP has radically changed its approach, causing it to blur the traditional line that segments the planning system and the ERP system. As a result, the planning system's role has been enhanced and the ERP system's role has been diminished. This strategic direction is evident in many small ways through the alternatives that are not made available for enlarging the role of APO into what are traditionally ERP activities.

Another question is whether or not planning vendors will adjust to SAP's design in this area. I pose this question because SAP is now so influential in enterprise software that they can drive the strategy of the best-of-breed vendors. Best-of-breed vendors may begin to develop views that allow client resources to convert requisitions to orders. If this were to happen, the integration would then bring in the data sent to SAP ERP or other ERP systems as orders rather than as recommendations, and planning systems will have significantly changed.

Additionally, some settings can control the flow of recommendations and orders from APO to SAP ERP in a dependent manner. Transfers of planned production orders can be set to only allow transfers to R/3 for planned production orders within the SNP production horizon, and this restricts the adoption of changes to SNP planned orders from SAP ERP. The default setting is for no filtering of planned production orders in SAP APO; that is, APO posts all planned production orders and changes that are sent from SAP ERP. To filter planned production orders as described above, this setting must be changed in the Global Settings to "Only allow transfer for planned orders in SNP production horizon," and not "Allow Transfer from SAP R/3 for All Planned Orders" as is shown in the screen shot on the following page:

Table View　Edit　Goto　Selection　Utilities(M)　System　Help

Change View "Global SNP Settings": Details

New Entries

Planned Order Integration

SNP Planning Profile　　SAP

Global SNP Settings

Profile: Active	Inactive
Plannd Ord.Integratn	Only Allow Transfer for Planned Orders in SNP Productn Hor.
SNP: Interch.	Product Interchangeability Activated
SNP: Simulat.Version	Activated
SNP:GR for Plnd Ords	Processing Time
SNP:Deall.Activ.	Consider Scheduled and Deallocated Activities
SNP: Scrap	Resource Consumption to Remain Unchanged
Aggr.: Old Orders	Delete at Sub Location Product Level
Agg: Order Group	Do Not Use Order Group
SNP Block Calc.	Deactivated
TS: Que. Proc.	Always Process in Background
TS: Max. Waittime	
TS: Aut. Update	Do Not Update Timeseries Automatically
TS: Enh. Locking	Inactive
Depl.:Lot Size Prfl.	Transportation Lane, Alternative Dest. Location Product
Depl.: Qty Display	Confirmation Date
Depl.: No Stock Trns	No Message
Depl.:Deletion Flag	No Message
Depl.:Unit of Meas.	Base Unit of Measure of the Product
Depl.: Pull Horizon	Message
TLB: Product Unit	Product Master
TLB: Order Change	Change
TLB: Pallet Loading	Same Product
TLB: Order Selection	Object-Based

More on the conversion of recommendations into orders is described in the article below:

http://www.scmfocus.com/sapplanning/2012/07/18/where-material-and-procurement-planning-occurs-in-sap-erp-and-apo/

Conclusion

One of the more straightforward timing topics that surfaces during an APO implementation is the timings which control the flow of data between APO and SAP ERP. The transfer settings from SAP ERP to APO tend to be set to near real time and are configured in the CIF under the CMF1—Create Integration Model transaction, while the settings for the transfer of transactional objects from SAP APO to SAP ERP is controlled by the Transfer to OLTP transaction, and can be set to periodic or immediate transfer (but also tends to be set to immediate transfer).

APO is an unusual supply chain planning system in that it provides an alternative to converting recommendations into orders in APO, rather than having this conversion activity take place in the ERP system. In fact, my impression is that SAP encourages clients to perform recommendation conversion in APO rather than in the ERP system. One good reason to do this is that the views in APO are superior to those in SAP ERP, which gives planners better "intelligence" when performing recommendation conversion in APO.

CHAPTER 8

Critical Timing Topics

What follows is a comparison between various settings that are some-times confused for one another, or that interact in a way that people may have difficulty understanding. My source for these comparisons is discussions on real projects where I worked as a consultant. Basing my books on my true project experiences makes the books as realistic, accurate and beneficial to the reader as possible.

In this chapter I will compare the following:

1. The planning buckets versus the planning update frequency.

2. The planning update frequency versus the manual adjustment frequency.

Planning Buckets versus Planning Update Frequency

One very common statement is that supply planning must be placed into weekly buckets. However, when one evaluates this statement, it turns out that there is not much supporting logic for doing so. What the company usually means is that they want to see the data in the Planning Book in weekly periods, which is of course a different topic all together. The articles below explain both how time bucket storage and time bucket display are performed and how they are not necessarily the same.

http://www.scmfocus.com/sapplanning/2010/02/24/the-storage-buckets-profile-and-the-planning-buckets-profile/

http://www.scmfocus.com/sapplanning/2011/02/22/why-supply-planning-order-batching-in-weekly-buckets-is-unnecessary/

As was described in Chapter 3: "SNP Horizons, Calendars and Timings," data can be stored and displayed in different time periods (that is in a month, week, day). Of course, the Storage Bucket Profile that is used must always be equal to or smaller than the Time Buckets Profile (i.e., the display), as one cannot display something in a smaller bucket than that in which it is stored.

Initializing the Planning Area

The same rule applies to the Planning Area as applies to the Storage Bucket and Planning Bucket Profiles, as has been covered already in Chapter 2: "DP Horizons, Calendars and Timings."

Weekly Display or Weekly Order Batching?

The requirement to show the supply plan in weeks in the Planning Book can be easily met by setting the Time Buckets Profile to weeks. However, this does not mean that the "planning frequency" is in weekly buckets.[2] A quick look at the APO Product View will show that regardless of how the Planning Book displays the ordering (as well as the detailed view in the Planning Book showing the order dates, which is arrived at with a right mouse click), the actual orders are created on a daily basis. Naturally an order cannot be created in a week; it must

---

[2] When I discuss update frequency, I describe the batch jobs that are set up in each module and that run on a periodic basis, which is how procedures (the SNP heuristic, the PP/SD Optimizer, CTM, DP forecasting methods, etc.) are usually run in APO. However, batch jobs are not the only way to run a procedure. Additionally, through interactive planning—such as through the various APO planner interface screens—planners can run planning procedures, normally for a small subset of the overall product location database. Read about how to do this for the SNP optimizer in the article below:
http://www.scmfocus.com/sapplanning/2011/12/20/running-the-optimizer-for-a-single-location-versus-the-sub-problem/

be allocated to a day. This is why SNP will almost always have a daily Storage Bucket Profile.

Notice the main display planning bucket is weekly.

SNP PLAN	Unit	23.09.20	W 39.2012	W 40.2012	W 41.2012	W 42.2012	W 43.2012	W 44.2012	W
DistrDemand (TLB-Confirmed)	EA								
Dependent Demand	EA								
Total Demand	EA		4,000	3,200	3,200	3,200	3,200	3,200	
Distribution Receipt (Planned)	EA		4,000	3,200	3,200	3,200	3,200	3,200	
Distribution Receipt (Confirmed)	EA								
Distribution Receipt (TLB-Confirmed)	EA								
In Transit	EA								
Production (Planned)	EA								
Production (Confirmed)	EA								
Manufacture of Co-Products	EA								
Total Receipts	EA		4,000	3,200	3,200	3,200	3,200	3,200	

Avail/ReqT	Fix	Rec/ReqQty	Unit	Category	Category Description	Product	Source	Destinatn	MTr	Start Date	Start Time	End Date
12:00:00		4.000	EA	AG	Purchase Requisition	22142	Vend	San Di	0001	27.09.2012	12:00:00	27.09.2012

..in the detailed view, the actual day is evident.

With a telescoping planning book (which has a mixture of different periodicities) and in the early portion of the planning horizon, the planning buckets will be in the same as the storage buckets, but this changes when the periodicity becomes larger. For more detail on this topic, see the article below:

http://www.scmfocus.com/sapplanning/2011/02/17/creating-telescoping-view-in-the-planning-book/

Of the four modules covered in this book, only DP tends to have a Storage Bucket Profile that is set at something other than daily. DP is typically set at weeks to decrease the data overhead that it must maintain. DP's forecast is then disaggregated to a day, which is controlled by the DP Period Split Profile, when it is released to SNP, so that SNP can work with the DP forecast. The disaggregation can be performed any way that is desired, as discussed in the article below:

http://www.scmfocus.com/sapplanning/2008/05/29/dp-period-split-profile/

The most common disaggregation setting is to evenly divide the forecast among the five days of the week. So if a forecast for a weekly bucket is 100 units, then Monday, Tuesday, Wednesday, Thursday and Friday would each receive a forecast allocation of twenty units. However, I have also seen clients that place all of the week's forecast onto the first day of the week, which is a way of ensuring that stock is on hand to build products. In cases where the forecast is skewed toward the beginning of the week and if the production order is scheduled for Monday or Tuesday, the procurement may not bring in the necessary input products until later in the week if the week's forecast is not put onto the first weekday.

Up to this point, I have primarily described the live planning runs. When simulation versions (which are not sent to SAP ERP) are used, or S&OP planning runs are generated, the Storage Bucket Profile and Planning Bucket Profile can both be more aggregated, although in my experience they generally are not. Companies tend to copy over their live versions for simulations or S&OP versions, and tend to not change and assign different Storage Bucket Profiles or Planning Bucket Profiles. As simulation runs are normally performed outside of the main operational workflow of the live system, optimizing the performance of these runs (which could be done by decreasing the time and storage periodicity) is not a real focal point.

The Planning Update Frequency versus the Manual Adjustment Frequency
Comparing the planning update frequency and the manual adjustment frequency is simple, but when doing the comparison, it's important that all project participants are clear on the translation of the terminology being used. For instance, when a manual adjustment is made to a forecast, some companies will say that they "forecast daily." From a systematic perspective, making manual changes would not be considered to be creating a forecast. (Of course, another factor is how often the forecast is released.) Manual changes can be made in forecasting (or supply planning, production planning, etc. at any time. (GATP is generally an online system and expected to provide almost immediate ATP responses to sales

orders, so it does not really fit in with this discussion.) However, when a procedure is triggered determines when planning is performed. For instance, if CTM is run both daily and weekly, then supply planning would also be performed daily and weekly. Most companies allow manual adjustments at any time, and manual adjustments, of course update the plan, although in a much less substantial way than when a planning run is performed. Let's take the example of reorder points. Reorder points can be set several different ways, and in SNP, how they are set controls how frequently they are updated.

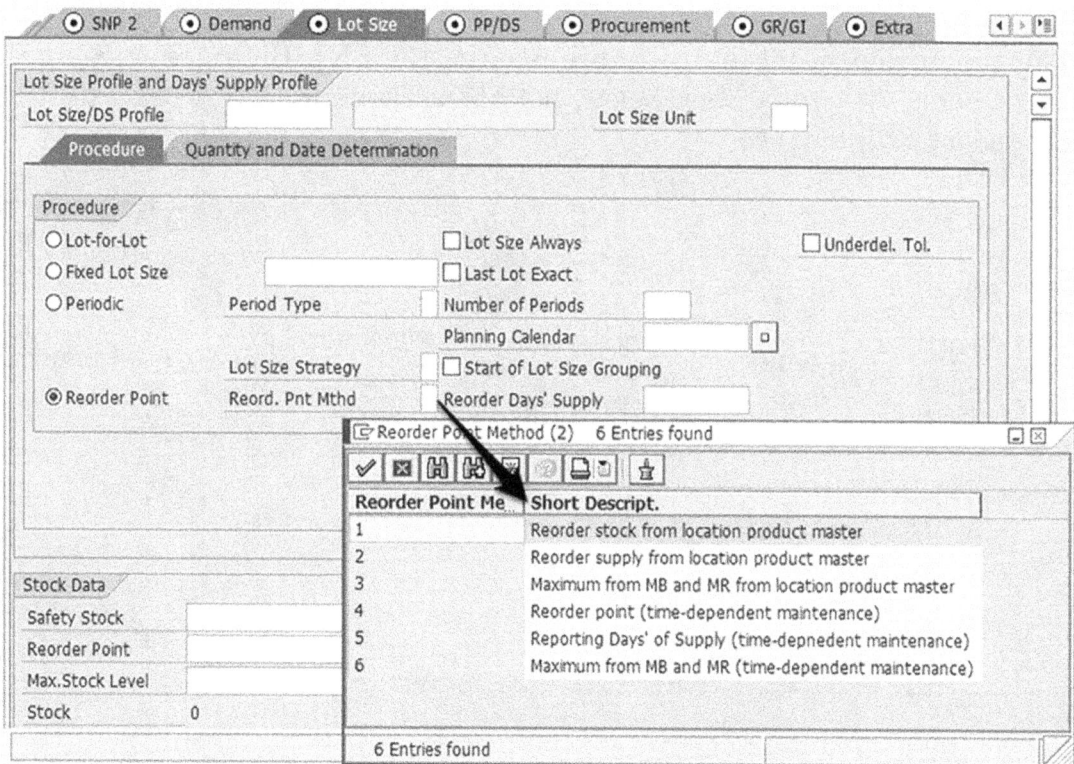

The drop-down from the Reorder Point Method field shows six different methods of calculating reorder points. The first three pull the reorder point from the Product Location Master, while the second three are based on time dependent maintenance, which means that they are variable along the time horizon (literally time dependent) and calculated in the Planning Book. With time dependent maintenance, the reorder point is calculated dynamically in the Planning Book.

This means APO creates an order based on the reorder point as soon as it receives information that reduces a planned stock-on-hand. (Unlike ERP, APO reorder points are based upon planned stock-on-hand. However, the macro that calculates reorder points can be adjusted to calculate the same as the reorder points in ERP.)

Therefore, there can be circumstances where a reorder point is recalculated immediately, or based upon running a procedure. The SNP Optimizer, SNP Heuristic or CTM creates a dependent demand, which results in the planned consumption of stock and in the planned stock level dropping below the reorder point.

When time independent maintenance is used, the SNP Heuristic triggers the reorder point. As can be seen below, not all methods in SNP work with time independent maintenance.

Reorder Point, TSL, TDS, Max Stock Level, and Lot Size and Major Supply Planning Methods						
(Major) Planning Method	Reorder Point	Target Stock Level	Target Days Supply	Maximum Stock Level	Lot Size (Units)	Period Lot Size
SNP Heuristic	X	X	X	X	X	X
Capable to Match						
SNP Optimizer				X	X	

Product Location Combination		Advanced Methods		Heuristic					
Product	Location	CTM	Optimizer	Heuristic With No Modifier	Reorder Point (Forward Calc)	Reorder Point (Non-Forward Calc) - Customized	Target Days Supply	Target Stock Levels
123	San Diego	X						
123	San Francisco				X			
123	Los Angeles			X				
123	San Jose					X		
567	San Diego	X						
657	San Francisco							X
Characteristics of Each Method								
Uses a Forecast?		Yes	Yes	Yes	No	Yes	Yes	No
Product is Forecastable?		Yes	Yes	Yes	No	Yes	Yes	No
Constrained Method?		Yes	Yes	No	No	No	No	No

Once a reorder point is triggered, it initiates a Planned Order, which can be converted to either a Planned Production Order or a Purchase Requisition. Depending upon how the reorder point is set, it can also trigger a Stock Transport Requisition. However, when these planning recommendations are sent over to the ERP system depends upon the Transfer to OLTP setting that was described in Chapter 7: "Transfer Timings Between SAP APO and SAP ERP." As for Purchase Requisitions and Stock Transport Requisitions, SNP is the end of the road in APO for these objects, and they must be sent to SAP ERP. However, the conversion of Planned SNP Production Orders into Planned PP/DS Production Orders depends upon the release strategy to PP/DS (if PP/DS is in the solution architecture). Planned SNP Production Orders are converted in the following ways:

1. Mass converted (with the heuristic SAP_SNP_SNGL)

2. Interactively converted

In both cases, the source of supply can be determined either in PP/DS or from the order that is to be converted.

Therefore, as you can see, there are a number of configuration settings that control when "planning" is performed, including the following:

1. When the recommendation is triggered. (When the reorder point creates a recommendation.) For reorder points it can be when the supply planning method/procedure runs, causing the dependent requirements to make the planned stock-on-hand drop below the reorder point. But it can also be caused by a change to the planned stock-on-hand that resulted from a change in a condition in SAP ERP. With time maintenance reorder points, no procedure needs to run, as the reorder points are auto-calculated by the reorder point macro.

2. When the recommendation is sent to SAP ERP (dependent upon the "Transfer to OLTP" setting—periodic, immediate).

3. When the Planned SNP Production Orders are converted to Planned PP/DS Production Orders (mass conversion or interactive conversion).

Therefore, the impact of manual adjustments on the overall plan has to do primarily with the frequency with which recommendations are passed to other systems. In some cases the recommendations are passed immediately; in other cases they can be passed immediately depending upon whether they are converted manually or interactively. However, while some reorder points can be triggered without a method or procedure, it is most consistent to use the term "planning frequency" to describe the running of an automated procedure. In cases where there is no automated procedure (for instance, where PP/DS does not use the optimizer or heuristics but simply allows planners to move planned orders in the Detailed Scheduling Board), it is best to describe the work schedule of the planners. For example, if the production schedulers perform their planning just one day per week, then the production schedule is weekly. At some point, the production schedule must be firmed and released for production execution. If the production schedule is firmed on a Thursday for the following week, then this would be described as a weekly planning process, even though no procedure is run in PP/DS. Regardless of what is determined in this area, manual adjustments to a plan—as I have intimated several times already—cannot be considered to be the planning frequency, which takes us into our next discussion: firming or fixing.

Firming or Fixing

Firming and fixing are interchangeable terms. Essentially, they are an order status that prevents the order from being changed by a subsequent planning run. Firming or fixing is a way of "solidifying the order." I prefer the term "firming," and firming is the more commonly used term in the industry and is better understood. For whatever reason, "fixing" is used in SAP APO, but I will use the term "firming" for the rest of this section.

When is an APO planning recommendation complete? On the surface, the completion of the APO planning recommendation may not appear to be related to system timings, but in fact it is. On one project in which I was involved, a custom interface was pushed off until well into realization because the client needed to understand the "end-to-end process" in order to properly specify how the custom firming tool would work. Firming determines when planning is complete for a recommendation and when the planning recommendation is ready to be passed to the next stage.

How Does Firming Work Between SAP APO and R/3?

> *Planned orders that are transferred from APO to R/3 are firmed in R/3 irrespective of whether or not they are firmed in APO.* — **SAP Help**

When the R/3 (SAP ERP) communicates the status of planned orders, they inherit the firmed status. Therefore, firming is partially a result of the process of moving planned orders to R/3.

Types of Firmed Orders
There are two types of firmed orders:

- *Output Firmed:* These are firmed through manual changes. The *Output firmed* indicator means that the order quantities of the product receipts are firmed. If this status is set to "firmed," the quantity of the order can no longer be changed or deleted during automatic planning, even if the requirements quantity has changed or no longer applies. This status refers to the order header firming in the R/3 System. Production order and purchase orders transferred from the OLTP system have the status *Output firmed* in APO.

- *Input Firmed:* These are firmed by the system. The *Input firmed* indicator means that the product requirements of an order are firmed. If the production process model (PPM) for the order is changed—that is, you change the quantity of a component—the PPM is not re-exploded for the order. This status corresponds to firming the explosion in R/3.

However, while the process of firming is different, once firmed, these orders are treated the same way by the system.

Where Firming is Set
Firming that is activated or configured in the system is set in the Product Location Master in several places. Here the terminology switches to "fixing."

Firming / Fixing settings

Fixing can be set individually for both production orders and stock transfers as is shown with the first order. However, both these settings only apply for the SNP heuristic and the SNP optimizer. Therefore, all SNP planned orders from previous planning runs that are within the SNP production horizon are fixed and not deleted. If fixing is not selected, none of the orders from the previous planning runs are kept. The stock transfers work the same way, which is of course the setting below Fix Production, called Fix Stock Transfers.

The third setting is (SNP Interactive Order Creation) No Fixing. If this setting is selected, orders that are created manually are not automatically fixed. Unlike the previous two settings, this setting also applies to CTM.

However, notice that the firming for purchase requisitions is not set on this tab of the Product Location Master. It is also not on the Procurement tab of the Product Location Master.

Is There Such a Thing as Semi-Firm?

One client asked me if it is possible to have a status called "semi-firmed." They desired this setting for the stage before "firmed." APO does not have this intermediate setting. Hypothetically, such a setting could be used for display purposes, and never connected to actual functionality. However, in terms of connecting such a setting to functionality, it is unclear to me how this would work.

Whether an order is firmed or not determines whether it can be deleted by the subsequent planning run. The system needs to know definitively whether it has the ability to delete an order. Therefore, there is a good reason that "semi-firmed" does not exist in SAP APO. However, while there is no "semi-firmed" status, a supply planning procedure could be set regarding how it deals with unfirmed orders and firmed orders. The SNP heuristic does not offer an option in this regard (read about this in the article below):

http://www.scmfocus.com/sapplanning/2011/02/04/level-of-bom-planning-in-the-snp-heuristic-and-low-level-codes/

CTM does offer two different ways of dealing with firmed orders, as can be seen in the CTM Profile screen shot on the following page:

http://www.scmfocus.com/sapplanning/2012/06/22/firming-in-apo/

Integrating the Timings of SNP and PP/DS

In terms of the integration of timings between the different modules, of all the projects I have been on, the connections between SNP and PP/DS draw the most interest and are in fact the most complicated. As I have discussed, GATP can be connected to PP/DS. In the vast majority of cases, SNP serves as the centerpiece module for planning connecting to DP, to GATP and to PP/DS. There is nothing particularly unique about this design with regard to APO. All of the other suites and individual non-SAP products work the same way. (The exception here is PlanetTogether, which actually combines production planning, supply planning, and even some available-to-promise into a single application. How PlanetTogether does all of this is explained in my book, *Constrained Supply and Production Planning with SAP APO.*) So we will now cover the most important time settings that allow SNP and PP/DS to work smoothly together.

SNP Production Horizon

The SNP Production Horizon is the horizon that divides the responsibility, in terms of time horizon, between SNP and PP/DS. Because SNP's most common implementation design is with production resources, a frequent question on APO projects is, "Where does SNP stop and where does PP/DS end?" There are several dimensions to how SNP and PP/DS differ with respect to planning production. One dimension is the time orientation of each module (discussed in Chapter 5: "Resource Calendars and Timings") that SNP and PP/DS each work with. SNP stops at the time granularity of the day, while PP/DS goes down to the hour. By doing so, PP/DS gets the information it needs to perform detailed scheduling, which is one half of the focus of PP/DS. Another dimension is how far out along the planning horizon each system plans. The SNP Planning Horizon is typically set to a year, while PP/DS is typically set to between two and four weeks. As a result, SNP will always include the PP/DS horizon. However, the SNP Production Horizon essentially disables SNP production planning within the SNP Production Horizon. SNP planned orders only begin on the first day outside the SNP Production Horizon, so if the SNP Production Horizon is set for three weeks, SNP does not create planned orders until after the third week. Most often, the PP/DS Planning Horizon is within this SNP Production Horizon. However, on most projects, the PP/DS Planning Horizon intrudes for a week into the SNP Planning Horizon. So if the PP/DS Planning Horizon were set to four weeks in this scenario, there would be a one-week overlap where both SNP and PP/DS can create a planned order. This can be confusing, because I have said that SNP will always be longer than the PP/DS Planning Horizon, doesn't the SNP Planning Horizon simply completely envelop the PP/DS Planning Horizon? The answer is that it does, but the SNP Production Horizon prevents SNP from creating planned orders within the SNP Production Horizon. Getting back to the topic of the overlap, it is ordinarily not a problem. In many cases SNP will have processed the time horizon before it gets to PP/DS for that week of overlap, so essentially PP/DS will come and process the overlapped portion of the planning horizon again. However, if planned orders have already been created, then PP/DS will have no need to create additional planned orders.

Extended SNP Production Horizon

The extended SNP Production Horizon allows manually created planned orders to be created within it, but prevents an SNP planning run from creating planned orders within the horizon. How the Extended SNP Production Horizon works is shown in the graphic below:

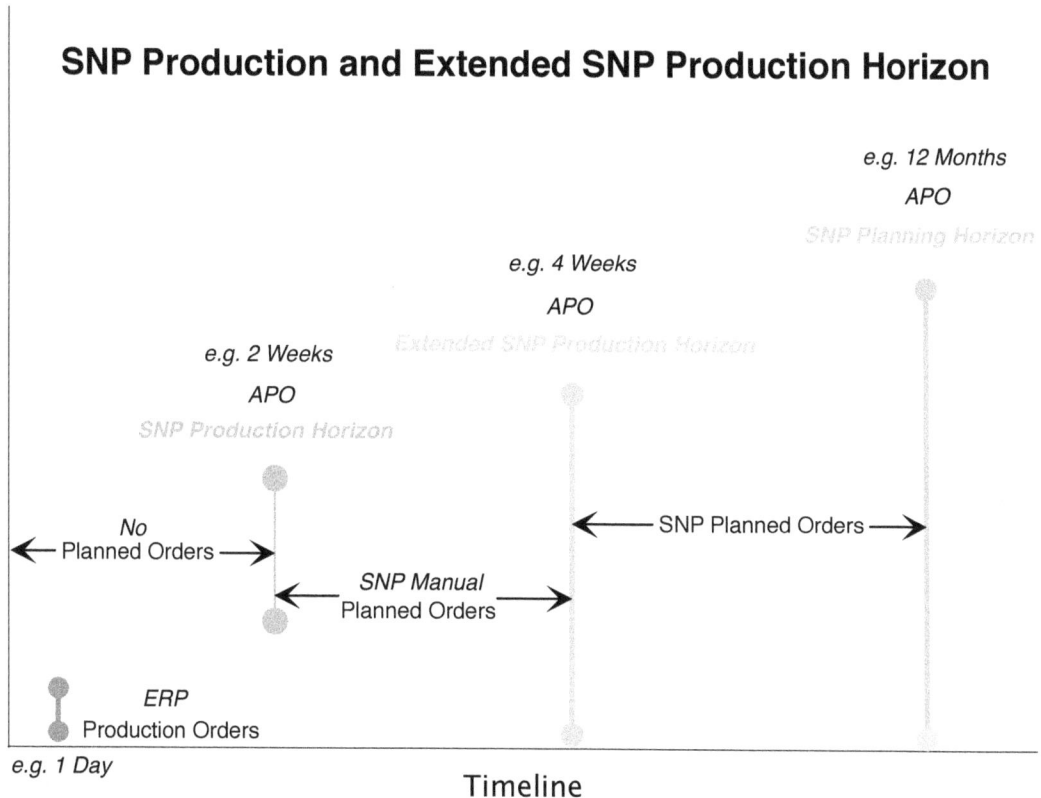

SNP Production and Extended SNP Production Horizon

e.g. 12 Months
APO
SNP Planning Horizon

e.g. 4 Weeks
APO
Extended SNP Production Horizon

e.g. 2 Weeks
APO
SNP Production Horizon

← SNP Planned Orders →

No
← Planned Orders →

← *SNP Manual*
Planned Orders →

ERP
Production Orders

e.g. 1 Day

Timeline

Conclusion

This chapter tried to clarify some timing topics that can be a bit confusing, which were the following:

1. Weekly display or weekly order batching.

2. Planning buckets versus planning update frequency.

3. Planning update frequency versus manual adjustment frequency.

4. When is a planning recommendation from APO complete (firming or fixing)?

5. Can orders be semi-firmed?

These are all important topics to clarify on APO projects. The implementing company may have very different definitions of what they mean when they ask any of the questions listed above.

CHAPTER 9

Timing Integration Between DP, SNP, PP/DS and GATP

One of the most important things to do on an APO project—or any supply chain planning project for that matter—is to differentiate between what the various timing settings in APO are doing, and explain how they relate to one another. To do so, one must understand what is created in each system and what is passed between the systems. This must be understood before the timing between the different modules is explained. The graphic on the following page lists the outputs of the different modules of APO that are discussed in this book.

Forecasts	Recommendations	Sales Order Confirmation	Recommendation	Orders
Results of DP	Results of SNP	GATP	Results of PP/DS	Results of ERP / R/3
Final Forecast				
	Planned Stock Transfers between Internal Locations in the Supply Network	Availability Checking based Upon Planned Recommendations from SNP.		Stock Transport Orders - Purchase Orders
	Planned (Production) Orders			
			Final Production Schedule	Production Order
Timing Demand planners focus 3 months out.	Supply planners focus on 2 months out.	Availability is checked up to 2 months out.	PP/DS focuses 3 weeks out.	Orders are created from two weeks to one day out.
User Interface Demand Planning Book	Standard Planning Book/Capacity Planning Book	Sales Order Screen	Detailed Scheduling Board	Stock Requirements List
	Product View		Product View	

In addition to explaining the output of each system, this graphic explains the relationships among the systems. Toward the bottom of the graphic the user interfaces are listed, which apply for each APO module. Secondly, examples of different timings that could be set for each module are listed on the timing row. These timings are simply examples of what they could be and must be customized per project.

This chapter will be broader than the other chapters before it. I will describe rules of thumb that can be used as shortcuts to understanding each of the comparison discussion points.

Controlling the Overlap with the PP/DS Planning Horizon and the SNP Production Horizon

Two horizons control the interaction between SNP and PP/DS. These are:

1. *SNP Production Horizon*: The period inside of which SNP does not create planned orders.

2. *PP/DS Planning Horizon*: How far out PP/DS creates planned orders.

The Background on Time Synchronizing SNP and PP/DS

A common question on APO projects is how SNP and PP/DS interact from a timing perspective. SNP will create the initial production plan—and in some cases a feasible production plan–when finite capacity planning is enabled on the resource and in the method. This production plan is then passed to PP/DS for adjustment. However, to work properly together, SNP and PP/DS must be synchronized in the following areas:

- When using CTM, the CTM profile must be set up for either time continuous or bucket resources, as described in Chapter 5: "Resource Calendars and Timings."

- The resources must both be selected (that is the right resource type used and configured in the right way) to support the integrated design.

- The SNP Production Horizon and the PP/DS Planning Horizon must be set up in a way that supports the design.

With respect to the horizon settings in the different applications, the following quote from SAP is instructive:

> *You separate the responsibilities for planning using the PP/DS horizon and the SNP production horizon. Planning within the PP/DS horizon is part of PP/DS planning and planning outside of the SNP production horizon is part of SNP planning, although the planning areas may also overlap.* — **SAP Help**

Therefore, the SNP Production Horizon and the PP/DS Planning Horizon can be set to the same value. This is applicable in situations when, in the design, the production planners simply plan and schedule what they are given by supply planning. Within the SNP Production Horizon, which can be seen as the stable or frozen period, SNP will not create any planned orders. In the opposite design, when there is significant overlap between the SNP Production Horizon and the PP/DS Planning Horizon, PP/DS and production planning can receive changes to planned orders within the PP/DS horizon. Furthermore, if this PP/DS Planning Horizon is longer than the SNP Production Horizon, production planners can move the planned orders between the weeks, or move them within a week.

*If, within short-term planning, you want to execute more detailed planning on receipts created by SNP, meaning that you want to plan them with detailed dates and a complete BOM, you must convert the SNP receipts into PP/DS receipts. PP/DS can either determine the lot sizes and sources of supply independently of SNP, or can copy the SNP lot size and source of supply decisions. — **SAP Help***

*You execute medium-term planning with SNP and short-term planning with PP/DS. The planning areas do not overlap, meaning that the PP/DS horizon and the SNP production horizon are the same length. If the SNP receipts reach the PP/DS horizon, you convert the SNP receipts into PP/DS receipts. — **SAP Help***

The SNP Production Horizon and
The SNP and PP/DS Planning Horizons

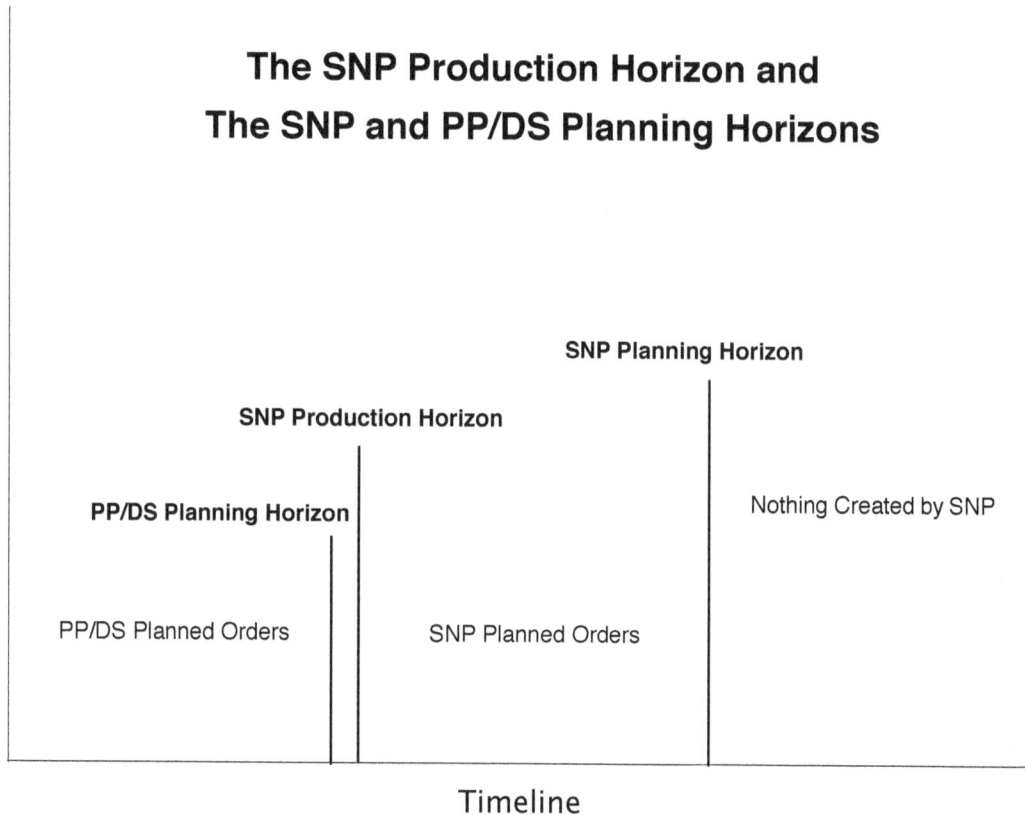

SNP Planning Horizon

SNP Production Horizon

PP/DS Planning Horizon

Nothing Created by SNP

PP/DS Planned Orders

SNP Planned Orders

Timeline

Here we can see when SNP is responsible for creating planned (production) orders and when PP/DS is responsible for creating planned (production) orders. The SNP Product Horizon can be seen as SNP's frozen period for the creation of planned orders. The SNP Production Horizon also controls the interaction with SAP ERP as can be seen in the graphic on the following page:

SNP Production Horizon and Planning Horizon

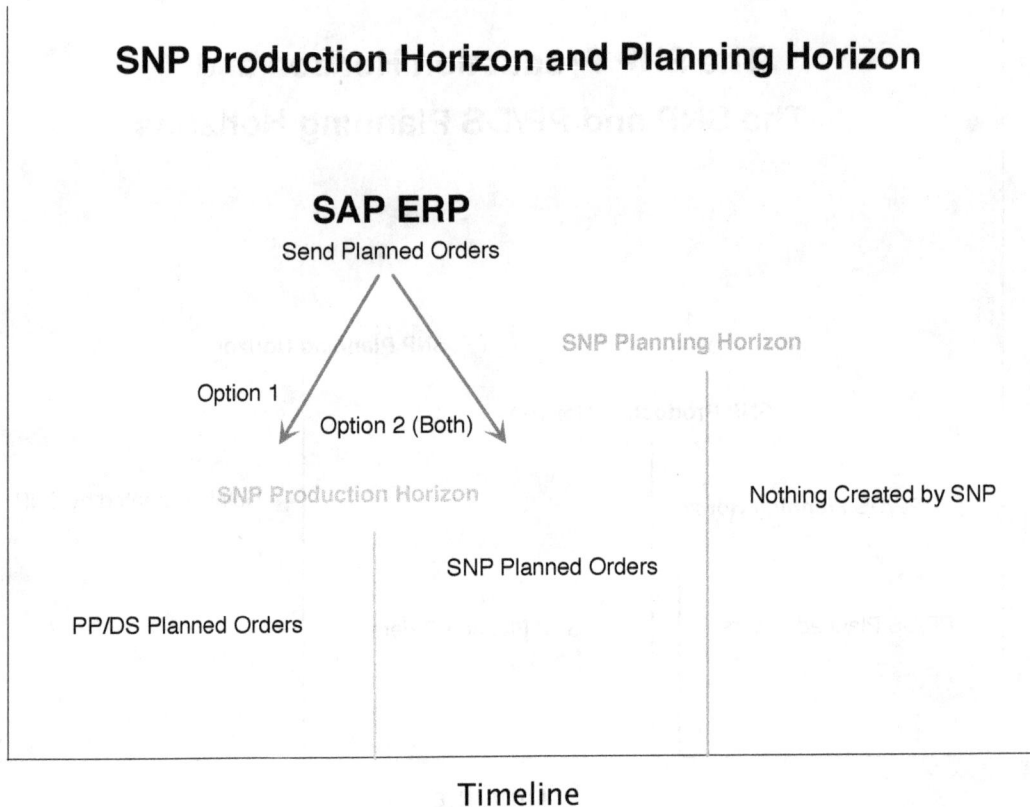

SAP ERP
Send Planned Orders

SNP Planning Horizon

Option 1

Option 2 (Both)

SNP Production Horizon

Nothing Created by SNP

SNP Planned Orders

PP/DS Planned Orders

Timeline

If you want the SNP Production Horizon and the PP/DS Planning Horizon to be the same, you do not have to enter a PP/DS Planning Horizon, as this quote describes:

> *You enter the PP/DS horizon and the SNP production horizon in the location product master for the products that you want to plan using SNP and PP/DS. If you want the PP/DS horizon and the SNP planning period to always follow each other without a gap, you only enter the SNP production horizon in the location product master, and no PP/DS horizon. The system automatically uses the SNP production horizon as the PP/DS horizon.* — **SAP Help**

This is shown in the graphic below:

Time-Continuous vs. Bucket-Oriented Planning

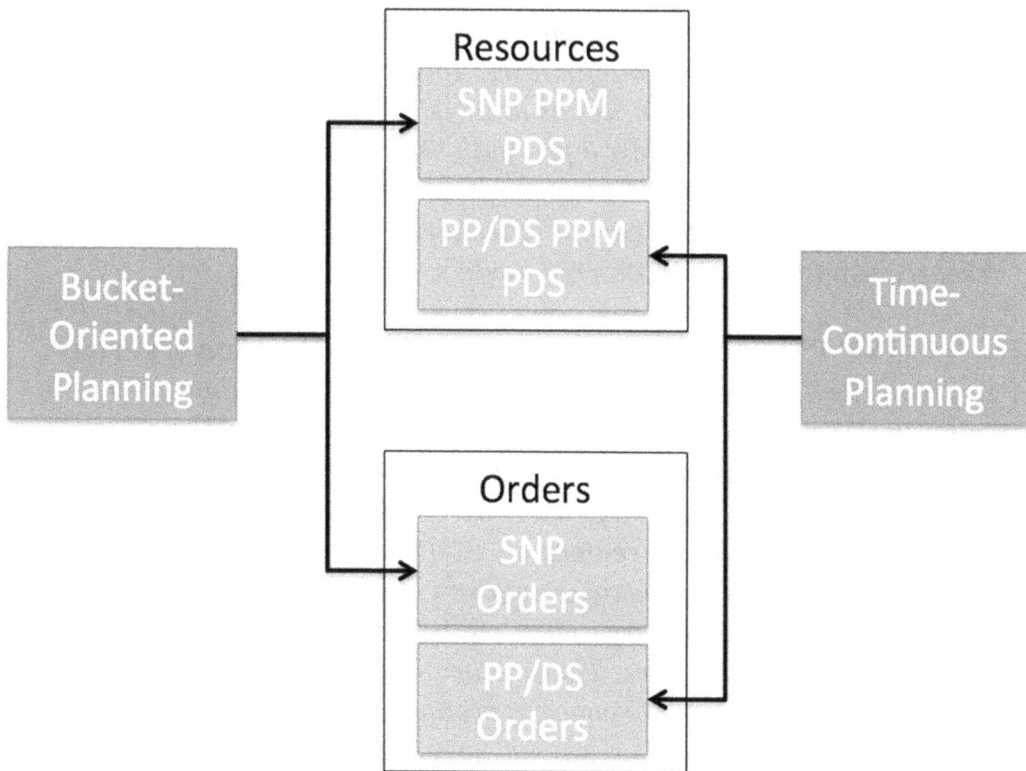

The Time Horizon Location Differences Between SNP and PP/DS

Another question can be about where SNP stops and PP/DS starts from the perspective of an individual factory. This is also a confusing aspect of these two applications, but much less frequently. SNP plans the overall supply network, and can be cognizant of production resources (although it should be stated, it cannot manage interactions between locations as does redeployment functionality).

I thought the following quotation from SAP on this topic says it well. SAP describes two different situations or configuration setups.

Where the SNP Production Horizon and PP/DS Horizon Do Not Overlap

Here, there is a common planning area for SNP and PP/DS in which SNP has planning control for certain finished products and their critical components; that is, SNP alone plans receipts and determines cost-effective sources of supply and lot sizes. You only use PP/DS to plan the receipts created by SNP in detail (that is, to complete the BOM) and to execute sequencing (for example, with setup time optimization). PP/DS copies the SNP source of supply decisions during conversion. For planning in-house production, this scenario requires the use of mixed resources and production process models. — SAP Help

Where the SNP Production Horizon and PP/DS Horizon Overlap

You plan the distribution centers with SNP and the production plants with PP/DS. You use the strengths of PP/DS (detailed production planning with complete BOMs and order sequences that are optimal for setup) for production planning. This degree of detail is not necessary for planning the distribution centers. In SNP planning, you only have to model the production capacities roughly in SNP to create plans that are also realistic with regard to production. SNP planning results primarily in stock transport orders. These orders are relevant to PP/DS if the stock transfer requirements concern production plants. — SAP Help

Within the PP/DS horizon, PP/DS can create receipts automatically. Outside the PP/DS horizon, you can only create receipts in PP/DS manually.

- *SNP plans outside the SNP production horizon, meaning that SNP can create receipts here. Planning within the SNP production horizon is fixed for SNP. SNP can no longer change an SNP order that has landed in the SNP production horizon. You have to convert it into a PP/DS order, if necessary.*

- *PP/DS receipts are visible for SNP as aggregated receipts, but they cannot be changed. SNP considers PP/DS receipts as confirmed production during the net requirements calculation. —* ***SAP Help***

Setup Times in PP/DS versus SNP

Setup times (the downtimes required for changing over to a new product on a production line) are maintained in PP/DS. However, SNP does not use setup times. SNP can only consider a constant setup time that is not dependent upon the sequence of products, meaning that PP/DS will have different times from SNP. This causes a discrepancy between the systems.

http://www.scmfocus.com/productionplanningandscheduling/2010/12/06/changeover-planning-in-sap-ppds-vs-planettogether/

Mapping Out the Work and Timing of Recommendations and Orders

In addition to setting the timings in the system, a company that is implementing the system must be shown when different things will be occurring in the system. This information does not need to be compiled from scratch because the company already has a timing and sequence in which they perform different activities. With the implementation of planning software, the timing and sequence must be evaluated to see if it needs adjusting. One of the best ways of doing this is to lay out a calendar in a spreadsheet. The calendar must cover days and weeks. A simple spreadsheet that has the horizons broken out graphically is a good way to start.

APO Planning Horizons

	Global or Local	Year 1 WK 1 WK 2 WK 3 WK 4 M2 M3 M4 M5 M6 M7 M8 M9 M10 M11 M1
Demand Planning Horizon		1.5 Years
GATP Order Checking Horizon		4 Weeks
SNP Forecast Horizon		2 Weeks
SNP Planning Horizon (Weekly Run) (constrained at the finished good for unconstrained)		1.5 Years
SNP Planning Horizon (Daily Run)		9 Months
CTM Time Stream		9 Months
CTM Demand Selection Horizon		2 Months
Pegging Horizon		2 Months
SNP Production Horizon	Product Location	4 Weeks
PP/DS Planning Horizon		Variable by Factory
PP/DS Planning Time Fence		
PP/DS Adjustment Horizon		
Deployment Horizon		2 weeks

Eventually it becomes necessary to get to a more detailed level, which breaks down the horizons by location—at least, for those horizons that can be defined that way.

I have included a sample spreadsheet in the image below:

First Draft Horizons

| Location Type | DC/RDC | RDC | RDC | RDC | RDC | RDC | Factory | Factory | Factory | Factory | Factory |
Location Name	Europe	Japan	Singapore	US - West	US - East	China	US	Germany	Norway	Time	Measurement
Demand Planning Horizon	21	21	21	21	21	21	21	21	21	Months	
GATP Order Checking Horizon	14	14	14	21	21	14	14	14	14	Days	
SNP Forecast Horizon											
SNP Planning Horizon (Weekly Run) (constrained at the finished good for unconstrained)	18	18	18	18	18	18	18	18	18	Months	
SNP Planning Horizon (Daily Run)	12	12	12	12	12	12	12	12	12	Months	
CTM Time Stream	12	12	12	12	12	12	12	12	12	Months	
CTM Demand Selection Horizon	We can flexibly assign per product.										
Pegging Horizon	12	12	12	12	12	12	12	12	12	Months	
SNP Production Horizon							21	14	7	7	Days
PP/DS Planning Horizon							28	21	14	14	Days
PP/DS Planning Time Fence							1	1	1	1	Days
PP/DS Adjustment Horizon											
Deployment Horizon	12	12	12	12	12	7	7	7	7	Days	

This spreadsheet can be used to gain consensus on what the various horizons should be. Notice that in this sample—which is drawn from an actual client, with some modification—some of the horizons are the same per location, while others are not.

The timing and sequence of activities do not have to be identical for all products. For instance, finished goods could be on one time and sequence, while components could be on another. Any other division of products can be assigned to different time and sequence models. This is the reason why placing the time and sequences into a spreadsheet, which can easily and precisely show the different "variants," is a good idea. A spreadsheet allows the time and sequences to be copied over easily, and also compared and contrasted. Getting to this final state means working through these timing and sequence variants with a group of business subject matter experts.

Conclusion

This chapter focused on timing integration between APO modules. Timing integration between the APO modules is one of the more tricky aspects of the overall timing setup in general. It can also be one of the less discussed aspects of projects as it is quite common for APO consultants to work in silos. Some of the APO time settings are really just module-specific, but the ones discussed in this chapter control how some of the modules interact. This chapter focused primarily on the timing integration between SNP and DP and SNP and PP/DS, as these represent the most complex timings among the four modules covered in this book. DP works very easily with SNP, and only a few timing settings are necessary to make the two modules work with each another. PP/DS is probably the more complicated of the inter-APO timing integration topics, especially as the PP/DS Planning Horizon can be set individually per plant. GATP integrates easily with SNP, with the accuracy of the supply plan, combined with the accuracy needs of customers being chief determinants in the length of the ATP Checking Horizon.

In most enterprise supply chain planning software, supply planning and production planning is a sequential process, with the supply plan created, sometimes with, and sometimes without production constraints. (Running the supply planning engine in either infinite capacity scheduling or with finite capacity scheduling.) The concept is that the planned production orders are sent to the production planning and scheduling system, and the planned production orders are sequenced by the production planning and scheduling system within the "buckets" assigned by the supply planning system. The supply planning system will often create a weekly plan, and assign the planned production orders to a week. The supply planning system then ensures that the raw materials arrive on Monday of the week, allowing production planning and scheduling simply to move the planned production orders around anywhere within the week. The production planner is often instructed to look out only one or two weeks when creating the production schedule. A reasonably good production plan can be created for a discrete manufacturing environment with a sequential flow between supply and production planning and scheduling. However, this is not the case with repetitive manufacturing, which requires a more interactive process between supply planning and production planning. Unfortunately, most supply chain planning suites offer a sequential process between supply planning and production planning, which can limit the effectiveness of many applications in repetitive manufacturing environments. I address a very innovative non-sequential design in the book, *Constrained Supply and Production Planning with SAP APO*.

CHAPTER 10

Forecast Consumption, Allocation Consumption, Scheduling Directions and Timings

In this chapter, I cover several settings that are similar in that they can be set backward or forward. Their brief definitions are included below:

1. *Forecast Consumption:* How the sales orders consume or reduce the forecast.

2. *Allocation Consumption:* How the sales orders consume allocations.

3. *Scheduling Direction:* How planned production orders and purchase requisitions are scheduled forward and backward in time from the day on which they would be scheduled given optimal circumstances.

We will start with backward and forward forecast consumption.

Backward and Forward Forecast Consumption

Backward forecast consumption means that current sales orders can go backward as many days as the system is configured in order to consume the forecast. Forward forecast consumption means the current sales orders can go forward as many days as the system is set in order to consume the forecast. The forecasts for prior periods are being applied to future periods, allowing the remainder of unconsumed forecast quantities to be consumed by periods of high sales orders. Forecast consumption occurs in SNP, and is set in the Requirements Strategy sub-tab of the Demand tab of the Product Location Master.

The fields on this screen are as follows:

1. *Consumption Mode: Controls the direction on the time axis in which the system consumes the forecast (Options are: Backward consumption, Backward/forward consumption, Forward consumption).*

2. *Backward Consumption Period: Defines the consumption period (in calendar days) for backward consumption. The consumption period is in calendar days not workdays. Since SNP and PP/DS can use different calendars, it is not possible to define a calendar for use with consumption. This may lead to unexpected results.*

3. *Forward Consumption Period: Defines the consumption period (in calendar days) for forward consumption.*

The Example

The mockup of the SAP Planning Book and its logic shown on the following page provide an example of where forecast consumption induces over-ordering. The overall orders that would be generated are compared both with and without backward consumption. The key figures without backward consumption are highlighted in light pink.

		Initial (Past 5 Calendar Days)	Monday	Tuesday	Wednesday	Thursday	Friday	Totals
	Actual Forecast	*6,000*	*2,000*	*2,000*	*2,000*	*2,000*	*2,000*	*10,000*
Demand	Forecast (*unconsumed forecast*) - with 5 day backward consumption		-	-	-	-	500	500
	Forecast (*unconsumed forecast*) - with no backward consumption	1,000	500	500	-	-	500	2,500
	Sales Orders		1,500	1,500	5,000	3,200	1,500	12,700
	Production or procurement orders with backward consumption		1,500	1,500	5,000	3,200	2,000	13,200
	Production or procurement orders with no backward consumption		2,000	2,000	5,000	3,200	2,000	14,200

Here we can see that the sales order of 5,000 units consumes unconsumed forecast from the previous periods. This adjusts the production or procurement orders down for Monday and Tuesday and may have also reduced the production or procurement orders from the initial column, depending upon when the sales order was recorded in the system. Secondly, the total order quantity with five-day backward consumption is closer to the actual demand for that period.

	Initial (Past 5 Calendar Days)	Monday	Tuesday	Wednesday	Thursday	Friday	Totals
Actual Forecast	6,000	2,000	2,000	2,000	2,000	2,000	10,000
Forecast (*unconsumed forecast*) - with 5 day backward consumption		-	-	-	-	500	500
Forecast (*unconsumed forecast*) - with no backward consumption	1,000	500	500	-	-	500	2,500
Sales Orders		1,500	1,500	5,000	3,200	1,500	12,700
Production or procurement orders with backward consumption		1,500	1,500	5,000	3,200	2,000	13,200 vs.
Production or procurement orders with no backward consumption		2,000	2,000	5,000	3,200	2,000	14,200

Forecasts have effectively been "pushed forward" to where they are consumed by sales orders. Using neither backward nor forward consumption promotes an upward bias in ordering. With backward consumption enabled, the total demand is closer to the actual demand. Without the ability to consume from other periods, the high sales orders on Wednesday will convert to production or procurement orders, but previous periods where the forecast was higher are not reduced.

One additional outcome of the backward consumption displayed above was to push the ordering forward to match sales orders rather than to match the forecast. While this outcome is not discussed often, it is beneficial. When forward forecast consumption is enabled, future ordering based purely on forecasts is reduced; however, only backward consumption postpones the orders generated to better align with sales orders.

Now that we have covered how forecast consumption works and its benefits, let's delve into some interesting questions regarding forecast consumption.

Implications to the Question of Backward Forecast Consumption

Here are some questions that should be discussed when explaining forecast consumption:

1. What is the purpose of forecast consumption in the same period? (In fact, one can set the forecast consumption to have zero forward and backward consumption, so that sales orders decrement the forecast only within the same period.)

2. What is the purpose of using backward or forward consumption? It is beneficial to observe (and also to describe to planners) that same-period consumption—and consumption that is either backward or forward—accomplishes two different objectives:

   • *Same-period Forecast Consumption:* This is intended to prevent double counting when calculating the total demand that will then be used to drive production, procurement or stock transfers. Same-period Forecast Consumption is one method of having forecasts and sales orders interoperate in a way that allows forecasts to serve as a placeholder for sales orders (forecasts are then gradually replaced by sales orders as time passes). However, forecast consumption is only one way to do this. There are at least two others, as I will explain in following section:

   • *Forecast Consumption Outside of the Same Period:* This is designed to prevent over-ordering. Over-ordering can occur when consumption is limited to the same periods by disallowing backward or forward consumption. While sales orders that are higher than forecasts are considered in the total demand calculation, sales orders that are lower than the forecast are not considered in total demand. Therefore, a forward or backward consumption setting (*or both, as both backward and forward consumption can be configured in most supply planning systems*) allows sales orders in one period to search and consume forecasts that have not yet been consumed in other periods. Products that are ordered more frequently tend to be given shorter backward/forward consumption durations, while products that are ordered less frequently tend to be given longer durations.

Alternatives to Forecast Consumption

There are several alternatives to forecast consumption that can achieve similar ends.

1. *Take the Greater of the Forecast or the Sales Orders:* One alternative method is to simply take the larger of the two values. In this way there is no forecast consumption; the forecast equals total demand until the sales orders exceed the forecast, at which point the sales orders equal total demand. The relationship between sales orders and forecast can change along the time horizon. For instance, some companies take the larger of the forecast or sales orders until five days out from the current date. At that point the forecasts are removed from the supply planning system, the logic being that only the sales orders should count when close to the execution horizon.

2. *Within a Certain Horizon Do Not Count the Forecast:* This method is actually another timing setting in APO called the SNP Forecast Horizon: Horizon in calendar days, during which the forecast is not considered as part of the total demand. Within this horizon, SNP does not take the forecast into account when calculating total demand. Outside of this horizon, the system calculates total demand using either the forecast or sales orders (whichever value is larger), and the other demands (dependent demand, distribution demand, planned demand, and confirmed demand). For instance, if the SNP Forecast Horizon is set to three weeks, then within this first three weeks of the SNP Planning Horizon, only sales orders count as demand.

Consumption in GATP

While SNP has forecast consumption, GATP has allocation consumption. In addition, GATP has a little-used functionality called forecast checking.

1. *Allocation Consumption:* Allocation consumption in GATP is where the sales orders consume the allocations. For instance, let's say a customer has an allocation of 100 units for a product at a location. If an order comes in for fifty units, the forecast consumption is reduced by fifty units. When a subsequent order for the same product at the same location for seventy-five comes through a week later, it will only be fulfilled for fifty units, even if there is plenty of stock or planned stock at the location.

2. *GATP Forecast Checking:* GATP also has something called Check Against Forecast, about which SAP Help has this to say: "*You execute a check against the forecast if you want to know if enough planned independent requirements are available for the incoming sales orders.*" When GATP is configured this way, the system essentially uses the forecast as the allocation. It is one way of configuring GATP, which in practice is not that commonly used.

Now that we have covered backward and forward consumption, we will move on to the next timing setting that can be set either forward or backward.

Backward and Forward Production Scheduling

Backward and forward production scheduling has more implications than backward and forward consumption. However, it is much simpler to understand because, while the primary goal of backward and forward consumption is to prevent over-ordering, backward and forward scheduling deals with "when" demand will be satisfied. Scheduling can be performed in two directions, but there are more than two options because the directions can be combined in one scheduling setting. Furthermore, different supply planning methods allow for different scheduling to be performed.

To understand how to use the different scheduling alternatives that are available in systems, it is important to begin with a definition of each of the scheduling types. SAP's definition of how the three scheduling options work in its system follows. These definitions apply for both SAP ERP and for SAP APO; however, other applications with supply and production planning functionality work very much the same.

1. *Forward Scheduling:* For the start date, the system uses the beginning of the period in which the production quantities were entered. From this start date, the system calculates in a forward direction to determine the finish date. The system displays the order quantities on the production start date.

2. *Backward Scheduling:* For the finish date, the system uses the end of the period in which the production quantities were entered. From this finish date, the system calculates in a backward direction to determine the start date.

3. *Backward/Forward Scheduling:* Here the system works in two steps:
   a. In the first step, the system uses the end of the period in which the production quantities were entered as the finish date. From this finish date, the system calculates in a backward direction to determine the start date.
   b. In the second step, the system uses the beginning of the period calculated in step one and then schedules forward. Order processing commences at the beginning of the start period calculated by the system and ends in the period specified by the planner.

Some systems such as MRP, which is the supply planning method in SAP ERP, are run with backward (then) forward scheduling by default. However, other supply planning methods, such as SAP CTM, do not have the ability to perform backward scheduling first and then forward scheduling, and can only perform either backward or forward scheduling in one planning run. Any supply planning system that is unconstrained must first perform backward scheduling. MRP is unconstrained and this is why there is no option to use only forward scheduling. SAP CTM has the ability to be constrained, and for this reason can be run with forward scheduling. In fact, with CTM, SAP does not offer the option to begin with backward scheduling and then move to forward scheduling, which is the default method of operation for MRP in SAP ERP.

More on backward and forward scheduling is available at that article below:

http://www.scmfocus.com/sapplanning/2012/06/27/backward-scheduling-forward-scheduling-sap-erp-sap-apo/

Backward scheduling is the most common scheduling direction. Backward scheduling works from the need date, and calculates the activities necessary to provide material availability "backward" from the need date. Forward scheduling works much more simply, and schedules activities to take place as soon as possible, as if the material demand date is immediate. Performing forward scheduling only in a supply and initial production planning run (and no backward scheduling), "front loads" resources (also known as "fill to capacity"). When applied to internally produced items, machine and labor resources will be employed to product material prior to their need. One might observe that this is wasteful, but in fact the activity can be the correct action to take. Companies do not build capacity to match the peak demand periods throughout the year. Some companies will find themselves unable to meet capacity at certain times, meaning that they have the option of producing early, producing late (if the customer accepts late shipments), or denying the order. Furthermore, the setup involved in some products is significant when compared to the inventory carrying cost of keeping the material in stock. One company I worked with was able to produce a full year's demand for an item in three hours, but the setup time to produce this item was four hours. It would not make sense for them to break the single yearly production run into two ninety-minute runs to avoid storing inventory.

Understanding the Primary Benefit of Forward Scheduling

Forward scheduling (also known as front loading) with internal production is primarily a trade-off between producing early and carrying inventory, or not producing early, and not filling one's production capacity. Forward-scheduling allows a company to produce and procure before the system would ordinarily schedule (meaning more inventory is carried prior to the inventory being consumed). Because companies typically do not have unlimited factory capacity or material availability and also because some factories—repetitive manufacturing environments in particular—require long production runs in order to achieve their potential production efficiencies, the ability to forward-schedule production orders and their associated purchase orders can be the correct approach to configure a company's supply and production planning systems. More detail on forward scheduling is available at the link below:

http://www.scmfocus.com/sapplanning/2012/06/13/front-loading-resources-in-sap-snp/

The forward scheduling setting can be seen in the screen shot on the following page, which shows SAP CTM in the Planning Strategies sub-tab of the CTM Profile.

The options that are available with respect to backward and forward scheduling are very important for the output of the planning run. For instance, a procedure that begins with backward scheduling, and then switches to forward scheduling (which is the default for MRP in SAP ERP) will produce a very different output than one that begins with forward scheduling.

Scheduling Direction and Its Implications

As I have discussed, forward scheduling can be the correct setting in some circumstances. However, effectively leveraging APO to meet forward scheduling means more than simply changing the scheduling direction in the supply planning method. For instance, setting forward scheduling with CTM can lead to an interesting result, which is shown in the graphics on the following page. It can mean that higher priority customers, whose orders are run through the allocation supply planning procedure earlier, can consume a production resource sooner than they would ordinarily with backward scheduling. Forward scheduling plans all requirements as early as possible, without consideration for when the demand is actually needed, as is shown in the series of graphics on the following page:

Before the CTM Run

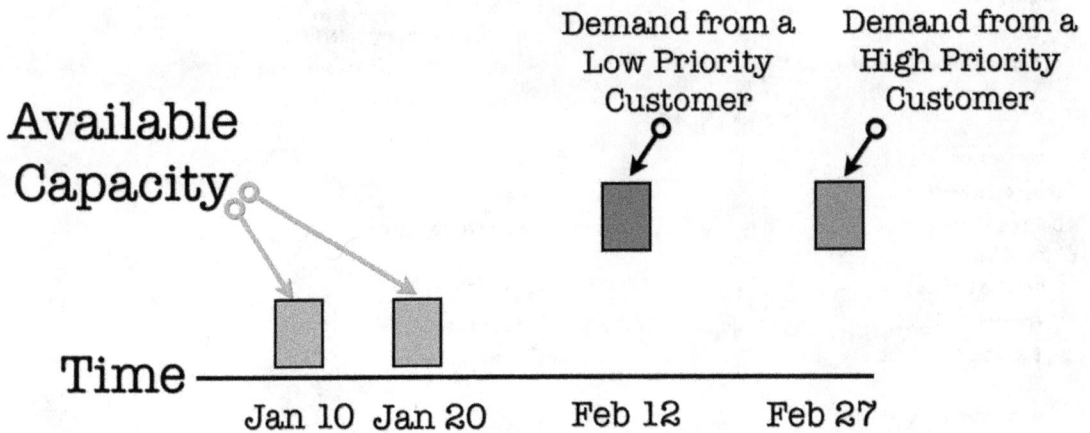

This is designed to show the state prior to the CTM run. Notice that there are two demands. The demand from the higher priority customer is farther out in the planning horizon than the demand from the lower priority customer.

The CTM Run with Backward Scheduling

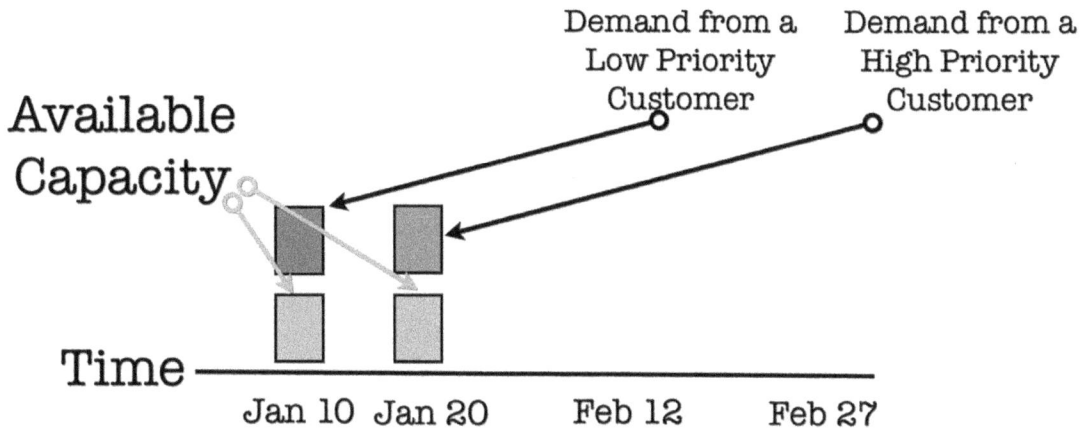

Under backward scheduling, as long as the demand from the higher priority customer can be met on time, the system will chose to peg or associate the demand with the later capacity.

The CTM Run with Forward Scheduling

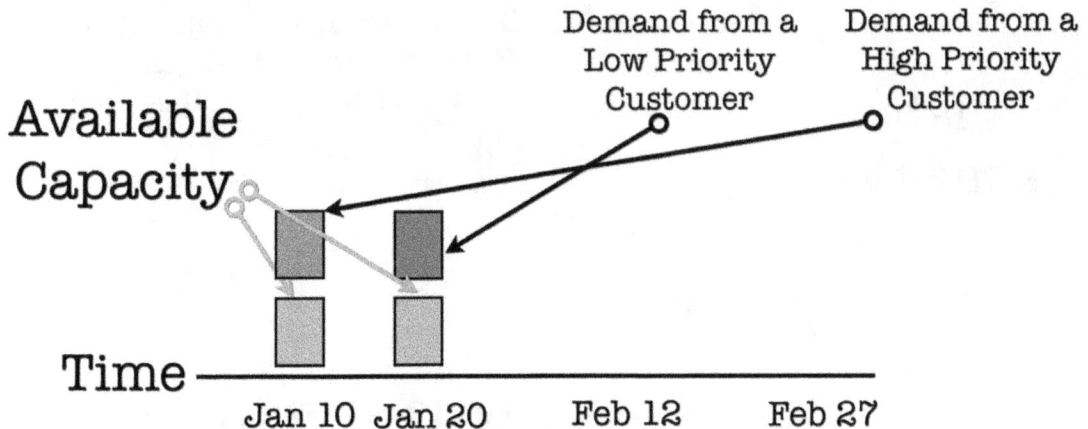

However, under forward scheduling, even if the demand from the higher priority customer can be met on time with the later capacity, CTM will assign the customer demand to the first available capacity. CTM does this because of the combination of CTM processing the higher priority customer prior to the low priority customer, along with the forward scheduling setting which plans all demands as soon as possible.

This is of course an undesirable outcome. However, there are several options, listed in the article below, to control this outcome and to prevent it from happening.

http://www.scmfocus.com/sapplanning/2012/08/08/effective-resource-front-loading-with-maximum-earliness-or-sequential-ctm-profiles/

Scheduling Direction When Using Cost Optimization

The supply planning method of cost optimization can also be made to perform forward scheduling. However, most often it will not have a setting for scheduling direction. Instead, the scheduling direction is controlled by the costs that are set up in the optimizer, notably the storage costs. Storage costs make the model incur a cost for each day that a product is kept at a location. The inclusion of storage costs therefore creates an incentive in the model to delay production until that product is required. Therefore, the use of a storage cost promotes backward scheduling. If storage costs are set to "0," many optimizers will immediately switch to forward scheduling. When storage costs are included, the optimizer switches to backward scheduling as it has now been provided with an incentive not to minimize inventory.

Backward and Forward Scheduling with Procurement and Stock Transfer Planning in SNP

Forward scheduling can be used to create planned production orders, purchase requisitions, or even stock transport requisitions prior to when they would be scheduled under backward scheduling. Companies routinely pull forward their procurement and stock transports in anticipation of future demand. Usually forward scheduling procurement and stock transfers are performed manually rather than set up in the supply chain planning systems. In order for forward scheduling to work in a way that meets the business requirements (and not simply initiate all activities immediately), it is necessary to constrain the resources over which the activities are spread.

In addition to demand spikes, there can be other reasons for forward scheduling. For instance, if suppliers are unreliable, then forward scheduling could reduce the risk of non-delivery or late delivery by creating purchase requisitions as soon as possible. Another reason for forward scheduling could be if the price of a material is predicted to rise in the future. Both situations can arise when an industry becomes capacity-constrained. Years ago this happened in the aerospace industry with titanium, with lead times becoming extended and so any part made of titanium was affected. In this situation, an alternative to forward scheduling is to adjust the lead times to make them represent the current environment.

As has been discussed throughout this book, it is common to plan with constrained production resources. It is much less common to plan with either supply planning resources (transportation resources, storage resources, etc.) or with the capacity constraints of suppliers (which would constrain the purchase requisitions).

The traditional output of a supply planning system is planned production orders, purchase requisitions and stock transfer requisitions (but as discussed in Chapter 7: "Transfer Timings Between SAP APO and SAP ERP," increasingly companies are converting recommendations in APO). Planned production orders and purchase requisitions are created by the initial/network supply planning run, and stock transfer requisitions are created by the deployment run. (I will cover forward scheduling in the deployment run shortly.) If the initial/network supply planning run is set to forward scheduling, it will forward-schedule planned production orders and purchase requisitions unless controlled in some way.

The scheduling direction for each supply planning recommendation type (production, procurement, transfer) should be analyzed and determined separately. That is, just because a company wants to front-load its production schedule does not necessarily mean it also wants to front-load or forward-schedule its purchase requisitions (for materials that are not part of a manufactured product) or its stock transfers. Therefore, the company must determine which recommendations from the supply plan they wish to forward-schedule and which they do not wish to forward-schedule, and then adjust the settings in the supply planning application accordingly. When it comes to the initial/network supply planning run, the decision of what to forward-schedule is quite important, because there are two types of recommendations (planning production orders and purchase requisitions) that come from this planning run, and the same scheduling direction may not work for both. Manufacturing companies may create purchase requisitions for products that are part of a manufacturing BOM, and also for products that are purchased and then resold. When forward scheduling is enabled and there are production capacity constraints, the purchase requisitions that are part of manufacturing BOMs will only be brought forward to the degree that there is manufacturing capacity. However, purchased materials that are not part of a manufacturing BOM will simply be brought forward as early as possible, unless the supplier's capacity is modeled and constrained. This is why it can make sense to place manufactured product along with the procured product that is an input to the manufactured product in one planning run and resold-procured product in a separate run.

Forward Scheduling in the Deployment Planning Run: Push versus Pull Deployment

Stock transfers are not created with the initial or network supply planning run, but instead by the deployment run. (They are also created during the redeployment planning run, but as SNP does not perform redeployment I will not cover redeployment reports. Nor will I get into non-SAP applications as this book is focused on APO. However, I do discuss redeployment in the following article:

http://www.scmfocus.com/inventoryoptimizationmultiechelon/2011/10/redeployment/)

Push and pull deployment is controlled in the following ways in SNP:

1. *By the Deployment Heuristic:* When controlled by either DRP or a common deployment heuristic, stock transfer requisitions can be based upon a push or pull deployment. When a condition at the receiving location (such as a demand or a target stocking level) controls the deployment, it is called a pull deployment. On the other hand, when the transfer is based upon moving material out from the sending location as quickly as possible, it is called a push deployment.

2. *By the Cost Optimizer:* A push or pull deployment can also be controlled by a differential in the storage costs between a sending and receiving location. A storage cost that is higher at the sending location rather than the receiving location creates a push deployment, as the SNP optimizer tries to minimize storage costs by moving stock out of the sending location before there is demand. The reverse situation causes a pull deployment.

I bring up the topic of push deployment because it is analogous to forward scheduling in the initial/network supply planning run. In a sense, stock transfers can be forward-scheduled through the use of push deployment, rather than pull deployment. This can be set up in SAP SNP in the SNP Deployment Profile, which is shown below:

Push deployment is set up for a number of reasons. The simplest reason is when there is only a small amount of storage space at a factory, which forces finished goods to be moved out immediately to a distribution center. However, push deployment, as with forward scheduling of the initial/network supply plan, can also be performed in anticipation of spikes in demand. Most companies know when these spikes in demand will occur, particularly seasonal spikes. Companies often do not build the capacity for their highest demand weeks or months into their supply network, and instead rely upon front loading or anticipatory stock transfers. Furthermore, a company can easily switch between push and pull deployment, as well as backward and forward scheduling, and therefore adjust its supply planning strategy depending upon the time of the year.

Controlling the Application of Scheduling Direction to the Product-Location Combinations

Supply planning methods can be controlled for selective product-based scheduling. In most supply planning systems, different master data profiles can be created that allow the planning procedure to be applied to specific subsets of data. For instance, procured products or manufactured products that do not need to be forward-scheduled would be placed in a separate profile with backward scheduling, or (first) backward (then) forward scheduling. All of this information should be maintained externally to the system in a product-location configuration database (which can be something as simple as a spreadsheet). This database allows analysts to compare and contrast more easily all of the settings that are applied to product-location combinations. This approach is described in the article below:

http://www.scmfocus.com/sapplanning/2012/07/04/product-location-database-segmentation-for-snp-and-supply-planning/

Forward Scheduling and Capacity Leveling

Forward scheduling can be used with an unconstrained supply planning procedure, but the unconstrained network supply plan must be processed with a capacity-leveling procedure. The SNP capacity-leveling heuristic can be run with forward scheduling as is shown in the screen shot on the following page.

Capacity leveling is the second step when a non constraint-based method is used for supply or production planning. As can be seen from the screen shot above, in SNP, forward scheduling is an option, which I have selected.

Scheduling Direction and PP/DS

PP/DS has several forward-scheduling heuristics that can be used to essentially do the same thing as has been described with forward scheduling in SNP.

1. SAP_PMAN_002 – Infinite Forward Scheduling: Compact forward scheduling in the event of a scheduling delay in make-to-engineer or make-to-order production, based upon today's date or an entered date.

2. SAP_DS_01 – Stable Forward Scheduling: Used to resolve planning-related interruptions using several BOM levels (infinite).

A full explanation of the heuristics available in PP/DS can be found in the article below:

http://www.scmfocus.com/sapplanning/2008/09/21/ppds-and-snp-heuristics/

However, the issue with forward scheduling in PP/DS is that these heuristics can only forward-schedule for the PP/DS Planning Horizon, which is typically not longer than a month. This is why forward-scheduling requirements tend to fall onto SNP, as it has a far longer planning horizon.

Conclusion

This chapter covered a number of time-related settings that can be set to backward, forward, or backward then forward. The intent was to show the reader the similarities between these settings, even though they are distributed across different APO modules. The following settings were discussed in this chapter:

1. Backward and Forward Forecast Consumption

2. Consumption in GATP

3. Backward and Forward Production Scheduling

4. Backward and Forward Procurement and Stock Transfer Scheduling

We started with backward and forward forecast consumption as one way of dealing with the interaction between the forecast and sales orders. This technique prevents the natural over-ordering bias that occurs when consumption is used in a supply planning system. In periods where sales orders are less than the forecast, the forecast is taken as the total demand. Backward consumption consumed previous forecasts, while forward consumption consumes future forecasts. Most supply planning applications allow forward and backward consumption to be used at the same time, and the distance (or number of days that forecast consumption is in effect) can be configured, as shown in the screen shot on the following page for SAP SNP.

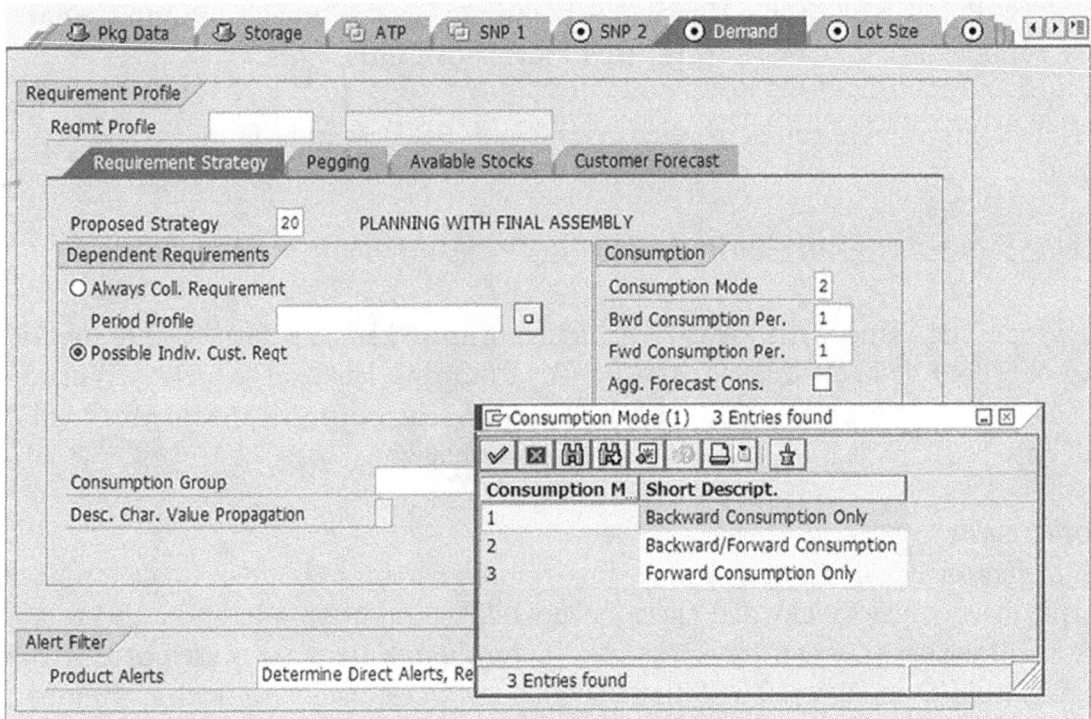

This screen shot shows how straightforward it is to add the scheduling direction and the length of forecast consumption. These settings are set in the Product Location Master in SNP and therefore are set at the product-location combination. This means that different combinations can have different forecast consumption settings.

Consumption and scheduling are important functionalities in supply planning systems. Because of their similar names, backward and forward consumption and backward and forward scheduling can sometimes be confused for one another.

Backward and forward scheduling is the implementation within the supply planning system of the company's policies with respect to how it will meet demand. The scheduling alternatives vary depending upon whether the supply plan (and initial production plan) is created in one step (that is capacity-constrained) or in a two-step (unconstrained) process, and these options also vary depending upon the system and the method that is used. For instance, in SAP ERP, MRP uses first backward then forward scheduling as the default scheduling method (also known as backward-forward scheduling). With the SNP capacity-leveling heuristic, forward or backward scheduling can be used. I show the SNP capacity-leveling heuristic screen below, which is set to forward scheduling.

Capacity leveling is the second step in the two-step (that is, unconstrained) supply planning and initial production planning run. Cost optimization applications for supply planning generally control the scheduling direction with storage costs, and not with a defined setting that is more straightforward to understand. If storage costs are set to "0," there is no reason for the system not to move the planned production orders as forward as possible, while still meeting demand.

Forward scheduling, when used with the allocation/prioritization supply planning method, will often serve to further increase the status of high priority customers over low priority customers. When capacity is available earlier and later—both of which would satisfy the higher-priority customer demand under conditions of backward scheduling—with forward scheduling, the first demand that is processed will be allocated to the first available capacity slot. This action will tend to build more inventory earlier, in some cases quite a bit earlier than it needs to be. However, adjustments can be made to control this outcome. The scheduling direction setting is very important and the same system with all the same configuration systems—except for different scheduling directions—will provide very different results.

One reason for using forward scheduling for manufactured items is to meet the needs of repetitive manufacturing, which must run in a relatively constant manner in order to attain potential production output and efficiencies. Other reasons for using forward scheduling include the need to pre-produce in order to meet spikes in demand or to batch the production for items with short production runs in relation to their set-up times.

Companies will often want to make scheduling direction decisions for their manufactured products and their procured products independently of each other, and if the decision is made to use a different scheduling direction for each, then the supply planning system can, in many cases, be set to incorporate different products into different profiles that are identical except for the products included in the profile and the scheduling direction. This is entirely controllable within the settings and the master data selections of many supply planning applications.

Not all products need to follow the same scheduling direction, and not all products need to be scheduled the same way through all times in the year.

CHAPTER 11

Conclusion

APO is the most fully-featured and complicated supply chain planning suite on the market. Its most widely-implemented modules are DP, SNP, GATP and PP/DS, the ways in which APO can be configured are unending, and with each new release the suite becomes even more complicated. This complexity generalizes to the timing settings, of which APO has an enormous number. Keeping them all straight, and associating the timings across the modules—as well as coordinating the timings with the connected systems—is a challenge. Furthermore, most projects do not include a Solution Architect who is responsible for integrating the APO modules with respect to timings and more, both with one another and with external systems.

Until one actually sees the timings entered in a system, planning horizons, calendars and time settings are difficult to visualize, explain and interpret. As a result, even experienced consultants often will put off the timing questions until the prototype or demo stage of the project. By the time that stage is reached, the software has been installed on a server, some basic master data has been set up in APO, and a connection has been established with the SAP ERP system so that both master data and transactional data can flow between the two systems.

The problem with this approach is that a considerable amount of project time will have elapsed before the timing question is finally addressed.

Generally speaking, software implementations don't become more efficient over time, due mainly to the disinterest in analyzing previous projects and rolling the observations of what to improve from past projects into future projects. For instance, the major consulting companies do not take a historical viewpoint when considering implementations, and thus do not learn from previous implementations nor focus on implementation improvement. There is little written on this topic. The articles below discuss the importance of analyzing the history of supply chain implementations to improve future implementations:

  http://www.scmfocus.com/scmhistory/2010/06/lessons-from-the-history-of-supply-chain-software-and-implementations/

  http://www.scmfocus.com/sapprojectmanagement/2012/05/top-5-tips-successful-implementation/

  http://www.scmfocus.com/sapprojectmanagement/2012/07/the-problem-with-sap-big-bang-implementation-approaches/

Throughout my involvement on many supply chain planning software projects, I have observed that supply chain software implementations can be improved by moving the discussions about timings to an earlier phase of the project. This book can help focus the project team's attention upon the timings as early in the project as possible. For instance, I recommend that the timings in this book be reviewed, and that several sessions with all the members of the various module teams be convened to discuss hypothetical timings that will eventually control the system. When such discussions involve both the module teams and the client—and take place early on in the project—everyone can start thinking about the right questions to ask and get ahead of the game on timing topics.

References

Babu, Mahesh. *Cross Plant Deployment.* Last modified May 14, 2010.
   http://www.sdn.sap.com/irj/scn/go/portal/prtroot/docs/library/
   uuid/20049b9f-e542-2d10-a083-d3cf60dde64e?QuickLink=index&over
   ridelayout=true&47515223697288.

Capacity Planning in Repetitive Manufacturing. SAP, 2001.
   http://help.sap.com/printdocu/core/Print46c/en/data/pdf/PPCRPREM/
   PPCRP_REM.pdf.

Conversion of SNP and CTM Orders into PP/DS Orders.
   http://help.sap.com/saphelp_em70/helpdata/en/c5/c4703736bfb37de
   10000009b38f8cf/content.htm.

Creating SNP Planned Orders from SAP R/3.
   http://help.sap.com/saphelp_scm50/helpdata/en/b3/32c5d32970834dad
   f53cac0aa2b5b4/content.htm.

Displaying the Product Availability Overview.
   http://help.sap.com/saphelp_scm50/helpdata/EN/c5/1a703760bf2d7ee10
   000009b38f8cf/content.htm.

Gaddam, Balaji. *Capable to Match (CTM) with SAP APO.* SAP Press,
   2009.

Hoppe, Marc. *Sales and Inventory Planning with SAP APO.* SAP Press,
   2007.
   http://www.sap-press.de/katalog/buecher/htmlleseproben/gp/
   htmlprobID-146

215

Integration of Purchase Orders and Purchase Requisitions.
http://help.sap.com/saphelp_scm50/helpdata/en/01/0d9d18a91011d5b4750050dadf0
791/content.htm.

Integrating SNP and PP/DS.
http://help.sap.com/saphelp_em70/helpdata/en/f1/c2d837ffbf2424e10000009
b38f889/content.htm.

Mass Production. Last modified January 8, 2013.
http://en.wikipedia.org/wiki/Mass_production.

Plant Stability. Last modified November 18, 2011.
http://www.help.apsportal.com/advanced-topics/multi-plant-and-multi-user-
settings/plant-stability.

Pradham, Sandeep and Pavan Verma. *Global Available to Promise with SAP:
Functionality and Configuration.* SAP Press, 2011.

Thonta, Srini. *SAP APO Global ATP.* Cogent IBS, 2008.
http://www.cogentibs.com/pdf/cogsap08/GATP.pdf

Vendor Acknowledgements and Profiles

SAP

SAP does not need much of an introduction. They are the largest vendor of enterprise software applications for supply chain management. SAP has multiple products that are showcased in this book, including SAP ERP and SAP SCM/APO.

www.sap.com

Author Profile

Shaun Snapp is the Founder and Editor of SCM Focus. SCM Focus is one of the largest independent supply chain software analysis and educational sites on the Internet.

After working at several of the largest consulting companies and at i2 Technologies, Shaun became an independent consultant and later started SCM Focus. He maintains a strong interest in comparative software design, and works both in SAP APO, as well as with a variety of best-of-breed supply chain planning vendors. His ongoing relationships with these vendors keep him on the cutting edge of emerging technology.

Primary Sources of Information and Writing Topics

Shaun writes about topics with which he has first-hand experience. These topics range from recovering problematic implementations, to system configuration, to socializing complex software and supply chain concepts in the areas of demand planning, supply planning and production planning.

More broadly, he writes on topics supportive of these applications, which include master data parameter management, integration, analytics, simulation and bill of material management systems. He covers management aspects of enterprise software ranging from software policy to handling consulting partners on SAP projects.

Shaun writes from an implementer's perspective and as a result he focuses on how software is actually used in practice rather than its hypothetical or "pure release note capabilities." Unlike many authors in enterprise software who keep their distance from discussing the realities of software implementation, he writes both on the problems as well as the successes of his software use. This gives him a distinctive voice in the field.

Secondary Sources of Information

In addition to project experience, Shaun's interest in academic literature is a secondary source of information for his books and articles. Intrigued with the historical perspective of supply chain software, much of his writing is influenced by his readings and research into how different categories of supply chain software developed, evolved, and finally became broadly used over time.

Covering the Latest Software Developments

Shaun is focused on supply chain software selections and implementation improvement through writing and consulting, bringing companies some of the newest technologies and methods. Some of the software developments that Shaun showcases at SCM Focus and in books at SCM Focus Press have yet to reach widespread adoption.

Education

Shaun has an undergraduate degree in business from the University of Hawaii, a Masters of Science in Maritime Management from the Maine Maritime Academy and a Masters of Science in Business Logistics from Penn State University. He has taught both logistics and SAP software.

Software Certifications

Shaun has been trained and/or certified in products from i2 Technologies, Servigistics, ToolsGroup and SAP (SD, DP, SNP, SPP, EWM).

Contact

Shaun can be contacted at: shaunsnapp@scmfocus.com

Abbreviations

(SAP) APO – Advanced Planning and Optimizer

APS – Advanced Planning and Scheduling

ATD – Available to Deploy

ATP – Available to Promise

BOM – Bill of Materials

(SAP) CTM – Capable to Match

CIF – Core Interface

DC – Distribution Center

(SAP) DP – Demand Planner

(SAP) ERP – Enterprise Resource Planning

(SAP) GATP – Global Available to Promise

DRP – Distribution Resource Planning

ERP – Enterprise Resource Planning

iPPE – Integrated Product and Process Engineering

MASSD – Not an acronym, but the mass maintenance transaction in SAP APO

MDM – Master Data Management

MEIO – Inventory Optimization and Multi echelon Planning

MOT – Means of Transport

MPS – Master Production Schedule

MRP – Materials Requirements Planning

OLTP – Online Transaction Processing

PDS – Production Data Structure

PPM – Production Process Model

(SAP) PP/DS – Production Planning and Detailed Scheduling

RDC – Regional Distribution Center

SAPGUI – SAP Graphical User Interface

(SAP) SCE – Supply Chain Engineer

(SAP) SNP – Supply Network Planning

S&OP – Sales and Operations Planning

(SAP) SPP – Service Parts Planning

(SAP) SD – Sales and Distribution

STO – Stock Transport Order

STR – Stock Transport Requisition

SYSID – System Identifier

TP/VS – Transportation Planning and Vehicle Scheduling

VMI – Vendor Managed Inventory

Links Listed in the Book by Chapter

Chapter 1

http://www.scmfocus.com/sapplanning/2013/01/17/saps-inconsistent-position-on-deployment/

http://www.scmfocus.com/sapprojectmanagement/2010/07/how-valid-are-saps-best-practice-claims/

http://www.scmfocus.com/sapprojectmanagement/2012/06/how-best-practices-expectations-causes-problem-on-sap-projects/

http://www.scmfocus.com/writing-rules/

http://www.scmfocus.com/

http://www.scmfocus.com/sapplanning

Chapter 2

http://www.scmfocus.com/sapplanning/2010/02/24/the-storage-buckets-profile-and-the-planning-buckets-profile/

http://www.scmfocus.com/sapplanning/2011/02/22/why-supply-planning-order-batching-in-weekly-buckets-is-unnecessary/

http://www.scmfocus.com/sapplanning/2010/07/01/planning-areas/

Chapter 3

http://www.scmfocus.com/supplyplanning/2011/10/02/the-four-factors-that-make-up-the-master-production-schedule/

http://www.scmfocus.com/inventoryoptimizationmultiechelon/2011/10/redeployment/

http://www.scmfocus.com/sapplanning/2011/10/12/snp-optimizer-sub-problem-division-and-decomposition/

http://www.scmfocus.com/sapplanning/2009/07/30/deployment-explained/

http://www.scmfocus.com/sapplanning/2010/02/24/the-storage-buckets-profile-and-the-planning-buckets-profile/

http://www.scmfocus.com/sapplanning/2011/09/23/transportation-lane-settings/

http://www.scmfocus.com/sapplanning/2009/06/20/transportation-lanes-in-scm/

http://www.scmfocus.com/sapplanning/2008/09/14/snp-transportation-lane-and-transportation-resource-setup/

http://www.scmfocus.com/sapplanning/2012/11/29/padding-the-transportation-lane/

http://www.scmfocus.com/sapplanning/2012/12/06/the-goods-receipt-processing-time-and-the-handling-resource/

Chapter 4

http://www.scmfocus.com/sapplanning/2008/09/21/ppds-and-snp-heuristics/

Chapter 5

http://www.scmfocus.com/sapplanning/2012/08/19/where-ppds-stops-and-snp-starts-with-respect-to-time-and-location/

http://www.scmfocus.com/sapplanning/2012/08/19/time-continuous-planning-versus-bucket-in-ctm-and-ppds/

http://www.scmfocus.com/sapplanning/2009/04/24/pds-vs-ppm-and-implications-for-bom-and-plm-management/

http://www.scmfocus.com/sapplanning/2009/05/03/scm-ppm-and-pds-as-used-in-different-modules/

http://www.scmfocus.com/sapplanning/2012/07/27/the-connection-between-boms-routings-work-centers-in-erp-and-ppms-pdss-in-apo/

http://www.scmfocus.com/sapplanning/2012/08/19/time-continuous-planning-versus-bucket-in-ctm-and-ppds/

http://www.scmfocus.com/sapplanning/2012/06/05/ctm-customer-priorities-versus-order-priorities/

http://www.scmfocus.com/sapplanning/2009/12/08/customer-prioritization-and-ctm/

http://www.scmfocus.com/productionplanningandscheduling/2010/12/06/changeover-planning-in-sap-ppds-vs-planettogether/

Chapter 6

http://www.scmfocus.com/sapplanning/2012/07/23/gatp-and-the-supply-plan-quality-and-the-order-promise-horizon/

http://www.scmfocus.com/sapplanning/2012/07/27/reorder-points-in-sap-apo-and-its-stock-calculation-method/

Chapter 7

http://www.scmfocus.com/sapplanning/2012/07/18/where-material-and-procurement-planning-occurs-in-sap-erp-and-apo/

Chapter 8

http://www.scmfocus.com/sapplanning/2010/02/24/the-storage-buckets-profile-and-the-planning-buckets-profile/

http://www.scmfocus.com/sapplanning/2011/02/22/why-supply-planning-order-batching-in-weekly-buckets-is-unnecessary/

http://www.scmfocus.com/sapplanning/2011/12/20/running-the-optimizer-for-a-single-location-versus-the-sub-problem/

http://www.scmfocus.com/sapplanning/2011/02/17/creating-telescoping-view-in-the-planning-book/

http://www.scmfocus.com/sapplanning/2008/05/29/dp-period-split-profile/

http://www.scmfocus.com/sapplanning/2011/02/04/level-of-bom-planning-in-the-snp-heuristic-and-low-level-codes/

http://www.scmfocus.com/sapplanning/2012/06/22/firming-in-apo/

Chapter 9

http://www.scmfocus.com/productionplanningandscheduling/2010/12/06/changeover-planning-in-sap-ppds-vs-planettogether/

Chapter 10

http://www.scmfocus.com/sapplanning/2012/06/27/backward-scheduling-forward-scheduling-sap-erp-sap-apo/

http://www.scmfocus.com/sapplanning/2012/06/13/front-loading-resources-in-sap-snp/

http://www.scmfocus.com/sapplanning/2012/08/08/effective-resource-front-loading-with-maximum-earliness-or-sequential-ctm-profiles/

http://www.scmfocus.com/inventoryoptimizationmultiechelon/2011/10/redeployment/

http://www.scmfocus.com/sapplanning/2012/07/04/product-location-database-segmentation-for-snp-and-supply-planning/

http://www.scmfocus.com/sapplanning/2008/09/21/ppds-and-snp-heuristics/

Chapter 11: Conclusion

http://www.scmfocus.com/scmhistory/2010/06/lessons-from-the-history-of-supply-chain-software-and-implementations/

http://www.scmfocus.com/sapprojectmanagement/2012/05/top-5-tips-successful-implementation/

http://www.scmfocus.com/sapprojectmanagement/2012/07/the-problem-with-sap-big-bang-implementation-approaches/